Praise for *The Ghost Horse*

"A heartwarming tale, artfully told . . . An easy winner."
—William Nack, author of *Secretariat* and *Ruffian:*
A Racetrack Romance

"*The Ghost Horse* will go down as one of the most irresistible horse-racing books ever written."
—Wayne Coffey, *New York Times* bestselling author

"I have always known that there were great stories at the race-track, but as a casual observer I couldn't really find them. They were buried under a culture and language that I didn't understand. So here comes Joe Layden . . . He not only has found a dandy story, he translates it for the rest of us and makes it sing. This is terrific stuff."
—Leigh Montville, *New York Times* bestselling author of *At the Altar of Speed, Ted Williams,* and *The Big Bam*

"Joe Layden manages to tell the story of Tim Snyder and Lisa's Booby Trap without undue sentiment, which demonstrates his respect for the story itself and the people (and the horse) involved in it. If some TV producer does get hold of it, he'll screw it up. Then Joe Layden will have to walk over to the shelf in his den, put his hand on the book and say, 'Nah, they never laid a glove on it.'"
—Bill Littlefield, *Only A Game* (PBS)

"Tim Snyder was a struggling journeyman trainer with a one-eyed, club-footed filly; not a likely combination for Thoroughbred fame, but in this case, at least, a recipe for a heart-tugging book. Joe Layden's sensitive retelling of a story about a man's love for a dying wife who promised that she would come back as a horse becomes a tale so gripping that even the most cynical racetrack tout will find himself touched."
—Barnes & Noble

W9-ATY-252

ALSO BY JOE LAYDEN

The Last Great Fight

The Ghost Horse

A True Story of Love, Death, and Redemption

JOE LAYDEN

ST. MARTIN'S GRIFFIN ✺ NEW YORK

THE GHOST HORSE. Copyright © 2013 by Joe Layden. All rights
reserved. Printed in the United States of America. For information,
address St. Martin's Press, 175 Fifth Avenue, New York, N.Y. 10010.

www.stmartins.com

Designed by Omar Chapa

The Library of Congress has cataloged the hardcover edition as follows:

Layden, Joseph, 1959–
    The ghost horse : a true story of love, death, and redemption / Joe
Layden.—First U.S. edition.
        p. cm.
    ISBN 978-0-312-64332-4 (hardcover)
    ISBN 978-1-250-02125-0 (e-book)
    1. Snyder, Tim, 1954 or 1955–   2. Racehorse trainers—United
States—Biography.   3. Lisa's Booby Trap (race horse)   I. Title.
    SF336.S69L39 2013
    636.1'235092—dc23

                                                            2013009269

ISBN 978-1-250-04864-6 (trade paperback)

St. Martin's Griffin books may be purchased for educational, business,
or promotional use. For information on bulk purchases, please contact
Macmillan Corporate and Premium Sales Department at 1-800-221-7945,
extension 5442, or write specialmarkets@macmillan.com.

First St. Martin's Griffin Edition: May 2014

10   9   8   7   6   5   4   3   2   1

Author's Note

While the vast majority of the information presented in this book was obtained through first-person interviews and original research, the author would like to acknowledge the following publications and sources for providing background material that proved useful in the writing of *The Ghost Horse*:

The *Times Union, The Blood Horse, The Boston Globe*, the *Daily Racing Form, Dateline NBC*, ESPN.com, Equibase, Finger Lakes Casino and Racetrack, *The Post-Star*, the *Herald-Leader*, the *New York Daily News*, the *New York Post*, the New York Racing Association, the New York State Racing and Wagering Board, *The New York Times*, the *Star-Banner*, the *Democrat and Chronicle, The Saratogian, Sports Illustrated, The Post-Standard*, the Television Games Network, the *Thoroughbred Times*.

Love, is always insufficient, always a lie. Love, you are the clean shit of my soul. Stupid love, silly love.

—William Kennedy, *Ironweed*

Introduction

SUMMER 2010

It was almost too good to be true.

A story about a one-eyed, clubfooted thoroughbred racehorse and the journeyman trainer who scraped together every penny he had (and borrowed what he didn't have) to purchase a broken and unwanted filly. And how the trainer helped the horse overcome its deficiencies, eventually naming her in part (but only in part, for the trainer was nothing if not complicated) after his deceased wife, the great and only love of his life—a bright and sweet-tempered woman whose gentle demeanor seemed eerily reflected in the horse. The trainer (and now owner) was by nature a crusty and combative sort, the yin to his wife's yang, a racetrack lifer not easily moved by new-age mysticism or sentiment.

And yet . . .

There were those final days back in 2003, when Lisa

Snyder lay in bed, her body ravaged by cancer, and tried to reassure those who loved her with a weak smile.

"It's okay," she'd say. "I'll see you again. I'm coming back as a horse."

Tim Snyder did not then believe in reincarnation. Truth be told, he still doesn't. But he acknowledged without hesitation the strangeness of this journey, the series of coincidences and almost inexplicable circumstances that brought them together, and the undeniable similarities between the horse and his late wife. So did those who knew the couple well, and who could now only marvel at the story of the filly, Lisa's Booby Trap, and the down-on-his-luck trainer who apparently had been given a new lease on life.

"You come across maybe four or five people in your life who are truly special, people who are genuinely good," noted Snyder's best friend, fellow trainer, and former employer, John Tebbutt. "That was Lisa. And I'll tell you something: this horse has the exact same personality."

The story of Lisa's Booby Trap developed quietly (and appropriately) enough in the relative hinterlands of thoroughbred horse racing, at Finger Lakes Racetrack in Central New York, where she rose from obscurity to win her first three starts against modest competition. But it really gained traction in the summer months, when the focus of the racing world, as it does each year, shifted to Saratoga Springs.

There are only a few places left in the world where horse racing is still followed and chronicled with the gusto of decades gone by; Saratoga is one of them. Each summer a sleepy little Adirondack town (population 26,000) springs to life, thanks largely to a massive injection of tourism that revolves around Saratoga Race Course. The ancient, wooden grandstand, with its elegant spires rising above a mile and an eighth oval, attracts an average of more than 20,000 spectators a day during July and August; for bigger races, such as the Travers Stakes, it draws as many as 50,000 people. The town's population swells in similar fashion throughout the sweltering summer months, with bars and restaurants filled to capacity, and the streets a virtual carnival, catering with great resourcefulness to a variety of folks—from the blue-blooded horse set residing in the stately mansions of North Broadway to the blue-collared workers who punch tickets at pari-mutuel windows, to the itinerant horsehands who live in near squalor on the backstretch and keep the machinery running smoothly, mucking out stalls, hotwalking horses, and grooming the stars of the show.

With the passing of Labor Day, it all comes to an end. The New York Racing Association shifts its base of operations downstate to Belmont, and Saratoga lets out a great, exhausted sigh before resting through the fall and winter months. For seven weeks, though, Saratoga Springs is the center of the horse racing universe, a minor league town with a major league sport. And in the summer of 2010, the star of the meet was Lisa's Booby Trap.

At first, like a lot of people, I followed the story from a distance. Well, not much of a distance, actually, as I am a Saratoga resident and my home is located roughly a mile from one of the track's two main entrances. In another life I used to work for the newspaper business, and I spent a lot of time covering Saratoga Race Course. I always felt that the racetrack, like a musty old boxing gym, was a good place to find an interesting story. There were characters aplenty, covering all levels of the social strata. There were men and women who had known unbearable hardship—for example, jockeys who starved themselves to death or vomited after every meal, or took speed and cocaine to maintain weight—and who persevered against ridiculous odds, often because they knew no other life, but also because of their genuine affection for the racing game and the animals at its center.

In short, they loved horses.

I'd heard a lot of great stories, but never had I heard anything quite like the story of Tim Snyder. And when Lisa's Booby Trap stormed down the homestretch a surprise winner in the $70,000 Loudonville Stakes on August 6, prompting the largest ovation of the Saratoga summer (and more than a few tears, as well), there was no choice but to get involved. It is, after all, what writers do. So I called Snyder and introduced myself, told him I was interested in meeting him and perhaps writing a book about him and his wonder horse.

"Sure," he said. "Stop by any time. I'm always here."

Indeed, he was. Although Lisa's winnings would later allow him to purchase two inexpensive claimers, Snyder at the time owned and trained just a single horse: Lisa's Booby Trap. Since he came to Saratoga as something of an interloper, Snyder had no barn of his own, but was instead given a single stall in the stakes barn not far from the Spa's paddock area (and a metaphorical mile from the pristine, multistall digs of superstar trainers such as Todd Pletcher and Bob Baffert). Although he still had a home (owned by his mother-in-law) back in Camillus, New York, not far from Syracuse, Snyder was essentially a wanderer, living out of his pickup truck and sleeping in a tiny tack room above the stakes barn.

When I arrived Snyder was seated in a rickety lawn chair not ten feet from Lisa's stall. With a wiry frame and skin like leather, and a cigarette dangling from his right hand, he looked every inch the racetrack vagabond. There was no pretense about him at all. He was a horseman, had been since he was born. Well, before that, actually. Snyder's grandfather was a trainer, his father a jockey. Some fifty-six years ago, while watching Warren Snyder ride at Scarborough Downs in Maine, Snyder's mother, Virginia, went into labor. Within a few hours she had given birth to a son, named Timmy, who entered the world in the track's first-aid room.

Snyder shared this story, along with countless others, while thumbing through a scrapbook of his life: pictures of his grandfather and father at racetracks throughout the northeast; pictures of Snyder at the farm he once owned with his wife, a blond-haired woman with a blinding white smile and a lean, athletic build. She was ten years younger than him, and from a different world. He was a nomadic but talented horseman who had trekked across the country scores of times, picking up work wherever he could find it; a rider who had gotten too big and broken too many bones to keep riding, and who had turned his attention to training. Cheap horses, mostly, that he churned to keep his little operation going.

She was a former show jumper who felt the lure of the racetrack and took a job as a hotwalker in her late twenties. They'd met one day in 1993 when Snyder nearly ran her down along the shedrow at Finger Lakes. She was young and pretty and Snyder fell for her instantly. Within two years they were married and in business together, eventually accruing a marginally profitable stable of twenty to twenty-five horses. They had a farm, bred and raised their own stock, bartered for others, and won their fair share of races at smaller tracks. Theirs was not an operation designed to produce or acquire Triple Crown champions. It was a way to make a decent and honorable living doing what they enjoyed most.

"Lisa was my partner," Tim said. "She was my wife. She was my best friend."

And then she was gone. Without her, he was adrift, literally and figuratively. He left home without so much as a good-bye, and spent the better part of three years on the road, self-medicating and steeped in grief.

"I didn't turn to drugs," he said. "Not much, anyway. But I drank a lot. Basically, I had a breakdown."

Each night, consumed by loneliness, Tim cried himself to sleep. Days . . . months . . . were passed in a near-catatonic state. It went on like that for more than three years, until slowly the pain began to recede and Snyder felt the pull of the only life he knew, a life at the racetrack. He returned to New York with nothing but his name and a fifty-something body still fit enough to gallop horses and clean stalls, and slowly pieced his life together.

It was less than the life he had, of course, but it was a life, nonetheless. He had support and friendship from his in-laws, and he had work, thanks in part to John Tebbutt, who knew of Snyder's skill with horses and was only too happy to see him return to the track. But even Tebbutt had to wonder about his friend in the winter of 2010, not so much because Snyder got it in his head to become an owner once again, but because the object of his affection was a big filly of modest lineage, with defects that left her owners and breeders disinterested. The horse was pretty to look at, seventeen hands high, with a glistening dark coat and bright white markings on her forehead. Somewhere in her bloodline there had been a bit of speed and a winning pedigree, but the filly apparently had been dealt a genetic short straw. She was sightless in her left eye and suffered from congenital abnormalities in her left foot and shoulder. One of her previous trainers had declared the filly to be the slowest horse he had ever seen. No one, it seemed, thought she'd ever make it to the starting line.

But they were wrong.

Like Shoeless Joe from Hannibal Mo, the middle-aged schlub who sold his soul for a chance to beat the *Damn Yankees,* Lisa's Booby Trap emerged from the shadows seemingly without notice or reputation, and took her sport, and the media that cared enough to chronicle it, by storm.

And then, just as quickly, and with even less explanation, she was gone, victimized by injuries or weak breeding or imprudent decisions by the horseman who loved her . . . or maybe just plain old bad luck. Some combination of all of those things, most likely. Horse racing, after all, is a brutal and unforgiving game, one that sidelines a large percentage of its most gifted athletes before they even reach adulthood.

Regardless, she went away, her trainer by her side, the two of them retreating to the margins of their sport, where happy endings wither and die.

Most of the time, anway.

Chapter One

Restlessness gets in your blood.

Whether by genetics or circumstance, the tug of the open road, the need to keep moving and changing, fighting the urge to settle down—to avoid getting close enough to anyone who might encourage roots to sprout—is felt more strongly by some than by others. In the case of Tim Snyder, it could certainly be argued that the odd romance of the racetrack life, as weird and nomadic as the circus it sometimes mirrors, was imprinted on his DNA, and reinforced at every step thereafter.

His grandfather, Earl Snyder, had been a reasonable man living a reasonable life in the rural hamlet of Duanesburg, New York, not far from Schenectady. The family had a small, working farm that required the combined efforts of parents and children to keep it viable. One day, though, as family lore has it, Earl took everyone to the racetrack and quickly became enamored of the life. In fairly short order he had sold off the farm, the livestock, and the equipment to tend them, and used the proceeds to purchase a single thoroughbred racehorse. Bitten badly by the bug, he moved the family to Belmont, New York, and embarked on a spectacularly dreamy and ambitious (if unfocused) midlife career change, one made even more complicated by the fact that it occurred in the thick of the Great Depression: he would be a horse trainer.

"My grandfather fell in love with horses," Tim Snyder said. "He couldn't help himself. And six months after they got to Belmont, his son—my dad—became a rider. A pretty good one, too. He was only fifteen years old at the time—same age I was when I started. But back in those days, I guess no one really cared how old you were—not even at a big track like Belmont. Long as you could get on a horse and hold him straight, you could ride."

Warren Snyder was a natural, small and lean, with firm but gentle hands, and an easy rapport with animals. Something else, too. He had a quiet confidence, the kind all jockeys have to some extent—after all, you need a sturdy sack in order to sit atop one thousand pounds of heaving horseflesh as it roars along the backstretch, in heavy traffic, at speeds of up to forty miles an hour. Not everyone is cut out for that sort of work. Very few people, in fact. But Warren Snyder was one of them, a gifted and aggressive youngster who didn't mind guiding his mount through cracks too narrow for sane or safe passage.

It's a truism around the racetrack that there are only two types of jockeys: those who have crashed, and those who are going to crash. It's also a truism that a jockey is never quite the same after he graduates from the first camp into the second. The ability to harness fear is a skill whose importance cannot be overstated. The "bug boy" (an apprentice jockey often still in his teens) rides with sometimes reckless abandon and a seeming weightlessness that is prized by trainers and owners and bettors, his mistakes and inexperience a fair trade-off in a world that covets speed and rewards risk, both at the window and on the dirt.

For a while, at least.

There is no shortage of stories about apprentices who lost the weight allowance that comes with the designation and soon thereafter lost their mojo, and then, naturally, the support of previously loyal and supportive handlers. Fear creeps into the equation, as well, fueled by failure or a stumble and the first chaotic, terrifying brush with mortality.

In short, for the rider, horse racing is easy. Until it's not. And then it becomes damn near impossible. A career that in its nascence seemed limitless suddenly becomes grounded in practicality and survival. Forget the Triple Crown; just get me a ride at Rockingham, preferably on a nag that won't start coughing up blood at the sixteenth pole or snap a tendon while I'm trying to squeeze by on the rail.

A jockey's career, like anyone else's, ebbs and flows over time, for any number of reasons. But the trajectory tends to be parabolic, and once the descent begins it's hard to slow it down. At the height of his career, Warren Snyder was a semi-regular in the racetrack equivalent of the major leagues, at places like Belmont and Aqueduct, where the horses generally are sound, the purses substantial, and the potential for fame and fortune tantalizingly real. Tim has photos of his dad, youthful and fit, sitting proudly atop his mount in the winner's circle at

Belmont, hordes of racetrack fans in the background, reminders of a time when life held infinite promise and horse racing ruled in the hearts and minds of American sports fans.

For whatever reason, Warren Snyder soon found himself in the minors, bouncing from track to track all along the Eastern Seaboard, but primarily at the hardscrabble tracks of New England—places like Rockingham Park in New Hampshire, Suffolk Downs near Boston, and Scarborough Downs in Maine. He rode regularly and with varying degrees of success or failure for more than three decades, eking out a living any way he could. When his body protested the starvation and other reducing methods imposed upon it, and he became too big to secure mounts, he'd do what any seasoned horseman would do: he'd pick up a few bucks as a hotwalker or groom. Anything to pay the bills and support the family.

Sometimes, though, he'd piss away the paycheck on booze or betting, and it wasn't long before promise and potential gave way to resignation.

"When people think of horse racing they tend to think of the glamour and the high level of racing at places like the Kentucky Derby," said Cheryl Hall, Tim Snyder's older sister. "But it's not like that for most people. It wasn't like that for Timmy and it wasn't like that for my father. But I want to make one thing clear: in neither case was it because of a lack of talent. It was because of the drinking. It's funny—Timmy and my father had so many issues with each other, and yet they were so much alike. They were both true horsemen who could have made different lives for themselves if alcohol had not been involved. Drinking changes people; it makes them unreliable. It causes a myriad of problems."

Added Tim Snyder: "My father was a well-known rider in some circles, but in the end, he was just a waste of talent, mainly because of the drinking. That's harsh, but it's the truth. I don't know . . . maybe he had reason to drink. He lost his family, his livelihood, everything, really. By the end he was broken in half. His life story was a story in itself."

Warren and Virginia Snyder were, by necessity, an itinerant couple, roaming from one track to another, and one town to another, occasionally expanding on the family in ways almost too weird for words. Cheryl, born in 1949, was the oldest. She slipped into the world slightly ahead of schedule, as her parents were driving to Oaklawn Park Racetrack in Hot Springs, Arkansas. The couple stopped at Harpers Ferry, Virginia, just long enough for Cheryl to be delivered safely. The newborn girl spent her first night on Earth sleeping in the bottom drawer of a hotel dresser that had been rigged to serve as a crib.

Six years later Timmy came along, dropping into the crowd at Scarborough Downs with all the urgency of a gambler trying to get a bet down in the waning seconds before post time. His mother was jostling with folks on the escalator at the time, rushing to join her husband in the winner's circle after he'd finished first in the last race of the day. She never made it, though, instead taking a detour to the first-aid room, where she gave birth to her oldest son. There would be two more children, Eddie and Danny, before Virginia Snyder called it quits. If the children had a sometimes chaotic upbringing, it was not without its charms.

"We grew up in the backseat of our cars," Cheryl said wistfully. "I can remember sitting there at night, looking out the windows, staring at the stars. We never really settled down."

What is normal, anyway? Tim Snyder never knew anything but the racetrack life, which was by definition an erratic, unpredictable existence. Through the eyes of an eight-year-old, though, it wasn't so bad. The places they lived—Old Orchard Beach, Maine; Salem, New Hampshire—were veritable playgrounds for a little boy, especially in the sultry summer months, at the height of the tourist season. In the winter time they'd pack up the station wagon and head south to Florida or Arkansas. Uprooting had its downside, of course—the kids were always changing schools, trying to make new friends, leaving old ones behind—but they leaned on each other in times of transition, or when things got ugly between their parents, which was not infrequent as the years went on and money got tight and Warren's drinking escalated.

It's strange the way things can sour. For a while Warren Snyder was a hot rider on the New England circuit, and though that didn't exactly make him Willie Shoemaker, it did carry with it a degree of notoriety that wasn't unappealing. But when things went bad, they went really bad.

"My dad would go anywhere to ride a horse," Tim recalled. "Maybe that's part of the reason him and Mom stopped getting along—because he traveled so much. That and the drinking, of course. In Florida he didn't just ride at the big tracks, he'd ride for the Seminoles on the reservation. Half the time they couldn't find my father because he was off living with the natives. He was a strange guy—didn't eat much because he'd get too big to ride, and so he'd drink a lot, maybe to fill his stomach, maybe to ease the pain. I don't know."

For most jockeys weight eventually becomes an issue, if not an outright obstacle. With age comes a slower metabolism, a loss of testosterone, and a natural thickening of the body. Bone and sinew give way to fat; injuries are slower to heal and result in diminished activity. An apprentice can eat almost anything, his body a veritable furnace of adolescent energy. The adult jock, though, must watch his weight and keep a careful accounting of his caloric intake, lest he find himself losing mounts because of excess poundage. With impending middle age, many riders find themselves facing a losing battle.

Knowing nothing else, and wanting only to hang onto the racing life, they fight anyway, using every weapon in the time-honored arsenal of reduction to keep their careers going. They do roadwork in rubber suits; they spend hours in the sauna; they gulp laxatives and amphetamines and coffee; they snort cocaine. Anything to curb their raging appetites. Sometimes they eat and retreat quickly to the toilet, where they heave their dinner before it has a chance to digest—a practice known in the business as "flipping." So accepted is this practice that some jockeys' quarters have a special stall designed specifically for this purpose.

Messing with the body's normal rhythm in this way has predictably nasty consequences, some physiological (tooth decay, heart arrhythmia), some psychological. You try going years without a decent meal and see what it does to your temperament.

"My father was always reducing, always starving himself, and that made him nuts sometimes," Tim said. "When he did eat, most of the time it was stuff he went out and found on his own. He'd spend hours hunting—pheasant and quail . . .

almost anything. And then he'd cook it and eat it. Or part of it, anyway. Funny thing, though: he loved animals. My dad wrecked more cars than I can count just trying to avoid running over a squirrel on the highway. 'Course he was drunk most of the time, so I guess that didn't help matters any."

Tim got behind the wheel of an automobile for the first time when he was barely in his teens, not because he was particularly adventurous or mischievous, but simply because the old man occasionally required someone to drive him around after he got loaded. You grow up fast in a dysfunctional family, and the Snyders were hardly the Brady Bunch. As the brood expanded, Warren became more inclined to travel on his own, whether for reasons of practicality, or merely because he craved isolation. Regardless, the separation was better for all involved.

"Dad was there sometimes . . . sometimes not," remembered Cheryl Hall. "When he was there, it was a very strict environment. My mother had too many children for my father's tastes, so it was uncomfortable when he was home. And he drank, which made things pretty volatile. So when he was gone, it was almost like a vacation. We did our thing, just me and my mom and my brothers, and everything was pretty good. She was a good mother—or tried to be, anyway—and it was quieter around the house. It was a generally healthy environment."

When Warren would return, though, tranquility gave way to turbulence.

"Mom was four-foot-eleven, and Dad was five foot," Tim said with a laugh. "And they would go at it like a couple of prizefighters, whipping on each other like you wouldn't believe."

Cheryl recalls the fighting with a bit less whimsy (she

was older, after all), and the combatants far less evenly matched or inspired. It was Warren who was usually the aggressor, the instigator, she said, and Virginia typically acted in self-defense. Both siblings, though, clearly recall an incident in which the fight spilled out of the house and into the driveway, with each parent screaming and flailing away, until Virginia finally got behind the wheel of one of the family's cars and began ramming it into the two other vehicles that sat in the backyard. Backing up, rushing forward, spitting dirt and debris and then crashing into the side of the car, creating a veritable demolition derby in the neighborhood.

Such outbursts, though, were rare for Virginia. She was more passive, more inclined to bottle things up until she couldn't hold the rage any longer. Repeatedly she threatened her husband: "Keep this up, and someday you're going to come home to an empty house."

Eventually, she would make good on the promise.

There was an accident.

It was one of many Warren Snyder endured during his career. Tim does not recall exactly when it happened. He was nine or ten years old at the time, and the family was living in Maine. Warren went off one morning to race at Scarborough Downs, as he had so many times before, only this time he didn't come back. Instead he wound up in the hospital. Warren had been riding near the front of the field when his mount buckled beneath him. Every rider fears being thrown from a horse; what they really fear, though—even more than death—is the prospect of a life-altering injury and years of pain and incapacitation. At no point is that possibility more likely than when a horse breaks down at the front of a pack.

"I guess it happened about seventy yards from the finish," Tim explained. "Bad spot to be in. He got run over by just about every horse in the field. Bunch of horses got hurt; his had to be put down."

There was a pause.

"My father had a rough life, a rough career. Lots of spills and broken bones. Always made a comeback. But this one was really bad—the worst that I can remember."

Warren Snyder spent several weeks in a hospital bed, trying to recuperate from a broken back and a compound fracture of the leg. Rehabilitative medicine in the 1960s was far from the science that it is today, and so Warren Snyder's care involved little more than rest and painkillers and antibiotics, washed down with whiskey or beer.

"It wasn't exactly upscale," Tim noted. "Doctors today seem like they can put anyone back together and get you back out on the track in no time. Back then they'd just operate and put you in traction. It wasn't long before he got an infection in his leg, and then he got really sick. Gangrene set in. They ended up drilling four holes in his leg: two pumping in fluid and medicine, and two others pumping the poison out. It got so bad they were thinking about amputating his leg. But my father was a tough little son of a bitch, and he wouldn't let them do it. You have to understand how hard it was to survive at the racetrack back in those days. It wasn't a sport for soft guys; still isn't, to be honest. But back in those days? Forget it. Whatever else he might have been, my father was a fighter. He refused to give up."

Then one day Virginia walked into the house and told the kids to pack their clothes.

"We're leaving," she said. "Now."

And that was that.

"We left everything behind at our house in New Hampshire," Tim remembered. "Everything except the clothes on our backs—and moved to Florida, and my father rehabbed his leg by swimming in the ocean."

Well, not exactly swimming.

Warren Snyder would limp to the shore with an inner tube in one hand, a six-pack of cold beer in the other. Then he'd drop into the hole, prop the beer on his lap, and begin paddling and kicking lightly out into the surf. In the beginning he was content to rock gently in the waves, slowly working his way through the sixer, letting nature's saline cleanse his wounds. In time, though, he began putting a little more effort into the process, methodically working his way up and down the shoreline. One day while playing on the beach Timmy noticed his father had disappeared from view, and he began to worry that maybe the tide had swept him away. A few hours later, though, Warren Snyder reappeared, a tiny, bobbing black dot on the horizon. It turned out he'd pushed the inner tube a few miles north, all the way to Hollywood Beach.

That became the routine for the Snyder family. Most days the kids would go to school, while Warren would trek to the beach. In time the leg healed—it took the better part of a year, but eventually he was able to walk on his own and even resume riding. After that, Warren Snyder made no secret of his contempt for formal medicine, and especially for the doctors who had told him he had a choice: lose the leg or lose your life.

The family stayed in South Florida for the better part of three years, as Warren continued to recuperate. Eventually he began picking up work around the track, exercising horses, hotwalking, whatever came his way. But economic hardship and chronic pain put a strain on the Snyders' marriage, which wasn't particularly strong to begin with.

"They all go together—injuries and painkillers and drinking," Tim said. "You take all that, throw in the fighting and the money issues, and the fact that my dad was half nuts at the time . . . there was no way they could stay together. They'd been hanging on by a thread for years anyway, and the injury pretty much sealed the deal."

When Warren Snyder felt strong enough to travel north and resume riding on the New England circuit, his wife and children stayed behind in Florida. Tim, as the eldest male in the house, took on an expanded role in the family, helping out with shopping and cleaning, and taking care of his younger brothers. By the age of twelve or thirteen he'd become an accomplished hustler (in the most positive sense of the term), shining shoes and selling tip sheets outside the front gate of Gulfstream Park.

He didn't really understand what had happened, didn't know that his father's exit had been permanent. Timmy had grown up in a state of flux: sometimes Dad went away, but eventually he always came back. Or they went to him. So there was no real explanation this time around, no big family discussion to frame a new way of life.

It just sort of happened. For the most part, everyone got used to it.

"Timmy was my mother's confidante," Cheryl observed.

"He missed out on a lot of childhood things because he became . . . almost like her partner. I mean, this was a kid who raced horses before he even got a driver's license. He was never a normal teenager; he was like a little man. He was so independent and such a big help to our mother. But I never completely understood the relationship and was always kind of jealous of it, to tell you the truth. All families are unusual to some extent. But ours . . ."

Cheryl laughed, collected her thoughts for a moment before going on.

"Our parents were off-the-charts crazy, honestly. Maybe that's a little too strong, but their lifestyle certainly was not the norm. My father was a racetracker and my mother had an art degree. They were sort of worlds apart. But she had that little wild thing going, too, and eventually that side of her personality came out."

Before long there was another man in the house, a military veteran who had served in the Vietnam War. Tim refers to his mother's relationship with the man as a "marriage," but that isn't true, according to Cheryl, since Virginia and Warren Snyder never officially divorced. To the children of a broken home, though, this was merely a matter of semantics. Tim knew only that his father was gone and a new man had taken his place. And while Warren was certainly capable of heaping abuse on anyone in the vicinity, including his children, at least there was a familiarity and predictability to his outbursts.

The devil you know, as they say.

"I didn't get along at all with my stepfather," Tim said. "We didn't see eye to eye. He wasn't my dad, first of all, but that wasn't it. He picked on me all the time, probably because

I was the oldest boy. You know—like a gunslinger; he always wanted to whip my ass. And he was really stupid and ignorant. Unfortunately, my mom thought the world of him, so she didn't do anything about it."

It's an old story, the one about the adolescent boy who rejects the new man in his home, the new man in his mother's life, without ever giving the guy a chance. But Cheryl Hall supports her brother's memory of that troubled time in their lives.

"Imagine what that's like," she said. "Your father is gone and everyone is trying to just get along, and there isn't much in the way of structure or discipline. Then all of a sudden this new guy comes along and he's all military and feels like everybody should be acting a certain way. Well, that isn't going to happen after living for so long without a father, and especially when it's coming from a complete stranger. We all rebelled like crazy."

In fairly short order the family had pulled up stakes and bolted for Key West, where Virginia's boyfriend had been stationed during the war. Cheryl, by now old enough to make her own decisions, for better or worse, got pregnant and then got out of town. She moved in with a girlfriend and their family, had another baby, and for a time lost track of her mother and siblings. But she never stopped thinking about them.

"I suppose I felt kind of guilty for leaving," she acknowledged. "But I had no choice."

By the time they left Key West, Timmy had fallen far behind in school. Ultimately, he would call it quits with nothing more than an eighth-grade education. The more settled existence the family had known since Warren had left gave way to pure transience. For a while they lived in Newport Beach, California, reuniting there with Cheryl, who was by now raising her young children and working as an interior decorator. Cheryl fell in love with the California coast and settled in for the long haul (forty-one years later, she still calls California home). Virginia, meanwhile, got antsy after only a couple years and hit the road once more.

"After they left California, they really started kicking all over the country," Cheryl remembered. "My mother had a little wanderlust in her; she liked to travel and move around and meet new people, and she became almost like a gypsy. She was a college-educated woman, somewhat conservative, but as she got older she became less and less constrained by society. She did a lot of things that I felt were wrong, and my brothers suffered in their childhood because of that."

While Tim is inclined to refer to his father as simply "an asshole," he chooses a slightly less pejorative term for his mom.

"She became a hippie, he said. "Every six months or a year, maybe two years at the most, we'd be on the move again. California, Oregon, Montana, Wyoming. We'd stop and pick fruit along the way, and not for fun! I mean, like migrant workers, the whole family out in the fields, me and my brothers, my mom and stepdad, all baking in the sun to pick up a few bucks. We did seasonal work—apples and pears in the fall, cherries in the summertime."

It was backbreaking toil, but Tim and his brothers did it mostly without complaint, for to raise a hand or voice an objection likely sparked an outburst from their mother's boyfriend, who had revealed himself to be every bit as much the belligerent and hostile drunk that Warren Snyder had been.

As Tim grew older and less fearful, though, he became less inclined to tolerate the abuse, and his relationship with the man naturally deteriorated to a point where violence was inevitable.

The way Tim remembers it, they were living in Yakima, Washington, at the time. The man had been drinking and an argument ensued. In fairness, Tim would later admit, it didn't take much to provoke his anger when he was around his mother's boyfriend. By now he was barely fifteen years old, and while small in stature he was wiry and strong, and virtually without fear. In some sense he actually welcomed the chance to spar with the big bully, and when things grew more heated Tim did not back down.

"I grabbed a jug of milk and broke it over his head," he recalled. "It was a bad scene. My mom was screaming, my brothers were crying, and my stepfather was bleeding all over the place."

What does a kid do in that situation? Does he wait for the police to arrive? Does he stay at home, knowing that retribution is inevitable?

"Couldn't do that," Tim said. "He'd have killed me."

So the boy grabbed a suitcase out of his closet, stuffed it with some clothes, and ran out the back door. He patted his brothers on the head before leaving, said good-bye to his mother, left them all crying in his wake. He couldn't have known, as he ran across the lawn and out to the open road, his chest heaving, his thumb extended, that he'd never see his mother again.

Chapter Two

I was born on a warm spring morning.

    Thank God it was warm—I couldn't imagine leaving my mother's nice warm tummy and entering into the world on a cold, dreary day. I was lucky. Some horses are born early and open their eyes to snow and wind whistling outside their stable. My barn was engulfed in sunshine by the time I took my first steps, and I enjoyed my first meal to the songs of the birds singing outside the window. In the meantime, my mom cleaned my ruffled coat and nickered softly, "Welcome to the world."

—Lisa Ann Calley
"One of a Dozen"

Some people merely claim to have had a lifelong love affair with horses, while others actually have the scars to prove it.

Horses, after all, are not like most other animals, and certainly not pets in the conventional sense of the term. They are big and strong and willful; they can be loyal or unreliable, prickly or affectionate. They are as unpredictable as they are majestic, their beauty stemming as much from inner mystery as it does from pure aesthetic. Spend enough time around horses, the true horseman will tell you, and eventually you'll get your heart broken; maybe something else, as well.

Carol Calley has a picture of her daughter on the back of a pony for the very first time. The little girl is perhaps four years old—maybe even younger—wearing a wide smile and a look of utter fearlessness. Inasmuch as it's possible for a child that young to express anything beyond basic approval or disapproval about her circumstances, Lisa Calley appears to be something of a natural. That image would only grow stronger, more vivid, as the years went on.

"Lisa loved horses, lived for horses," her mother would later explain. "She loved children, too, but she could never have any of her own. I think she always looked at her horses as being like her babies."

Frank and Carol Calley raised their two children in Central New York, first in the Finger Lakes resort town of Skaneateles, and later in Camillus. Frank was a hardworking and resourceful small business owner, while Carol was a stay-at-home mom. As mothers and daughters sometimes do, Carol and Lisa bonded deeply through common interests, in their case a fondness for horses. Within a few years of sitting on her first pony, Lisa was taking equestrian lessons, entering show-jumping competitions, and taking care of her own animals. There was a barn in the back of the house with stalls and a walking ring, where Lisa would spend every available moment.

"She was a joy," Carol said of her daughter. "I know, every parent says that about their kids, but we really were blessed. Both of our kids were exceptionally kind and gentle. I was closer to my daughter simply because of the horses. That became our thing, something for us to do together. I enjoyed it, but Lisa absolutely lived for it. She was never happier than when she was out in the barn working with her horses."

Even as a little girl, Lisa felt almost preternaturally comfortable around the animals. The normal and even healthy sense of trepidation and caution a typical child would experience was simply unknown to her. She felt a kinship to her horses, never feared them or worried that something might go wrong. It wasn't that she didn't respect the animals' strength or willfulness; she just saw these things as traits to be admired. They were part of what made the horses beautiful.

Accidents happen, even to the best and most experienced of horsemen. You can't live your life in fear, or beat yourself up after the fact. Carol Calley has reminded herself of this fact many times over the years, often with her daughter's voice in her head.

Lisa was eleven years old when it happened. She and her mother were finishing a typical day, leading the horses back into the barn, prepping another cycle of grooming and feeding and watering. Carol didn't see exactly what transpired, for Lisa was a short distance in front of her. She heard a commotion, saw movement ahead of her. Then everything stopped. When Carol reached her daughter, Lisa was on her feet, holding the reins of a quarterhorse named Misty, one of her favorites. The animal seemed agitated, but under control; Lisa was oddly quiet, a bit disoriented.

"What happened?" Carol asked.

Lisa squinted, gave the horse a gentle pat.

"He bucked."

There was little at the scene to suggest that Lisa had been seriously hurt, but something in the girl's demeanor—a lack of energy, a pensiveness—concerned Carol. Her mother's instinct kicked in.

"Honey, are you okay?"

Lisa stared blankly.

"I'm kind of groggy."

Later they would learn the details of the accident, or as many of the details as Lisa could recall. While entering the barn, Lisa had decided to jump aboard Misty. That, of course, violated protocol (not to mention parental rules). Lisa was always told to walk the horses through the barn and never to ride alone. Usually, if not always, she adhered to the guidelines. This time, though, she had decided to hop aboard Misty, who was wearing only a halter, for the final leg of the journey.

"She was kind of a bold person," Carol recalled with a smile. "Not in a disrespectful sort of way, but in a courageous way. She wasn't afraid of very much, even when she should have been. Jumping on that horse was a silly thing to do, but Lisa had been riding almost since she could walk—she never thought about getting hurt. She was always carefree and happy, maybe even a little reckless. If she felt like doing something, she'd do it. I'm not sure where that came from. Not from me, I know that. I always think of the consequences."

The horse rebelled instantly and tossed the little girl into a beam. Lisa, who was not wearing a helmet at the time, struck her head. By the time her mother arrived, though, she seemed to have weathered the incident without serious injury, if any injury at all.

She was tired, a little queasy . . . but nothing more. There were no cuts or broken bones, not even a bump or bruise. They finished their chores, closed up the barn, and went back into the house.

"At first she seemed okay," Carol said. "But after a little while she started complaining of a headache and said she felt like she was going to throw up. Then she got really sleepy."

The telltale signs of a concussion were not lost on Lisa's parents; the fact that she seemed to be only mildly impaired did not provide enough comfort to prevent them from taking her to a local hospital near Skaneatles. Emergency room physicians dutifully examined the little girl, taking X-rays and checking off each potential box in descending order of diagnostic concern.

They found nothing.

Meanwhile, Lisa grew more lethargic and nauseous. Eventually one of the doctors suggested to the Calleys that Lisa be examined by a specialist. As this was a small, lightly staffed community facility, they did not have a neurosurgeon or neurologist on site at the time. They suggested Lisa be transported by ambulance to St. Joseph's Hopsital, a much larger health center located roughly thirty miles away, in Syracuse.

"Thank God for that," Carol recalled. "If we'd waited, or just gone home, I don't know what might have happened."

By the time the family arrived at St. Joe's, Lisa's X-rays and CAT scans had already been transmitted. A neurosurgeon was waiting for them, with a surgical suite prepared. Lisa had sustained a serious hematoma to the skull, which was rapidly filling with fluid and putting pressure on her brain. By the time they wheeled her into surgery, the lump had expanded to the size of a lemon.

"She could have died in her home, or in the barn," Carol said. "She could have died on the way to the hospital. We had no idea at the time just how serious it was."

Fighter that she was (a designation she would prove repeatedly in the coming years), Lisa pulled through the surgery without incident and recovered in fairly short order. Had it been left up to Frank Calley, Misty would have been destroyed (humanely or otherwise) before Lisa even came home from the hospital. Lisa wouldn't stand for it. At first she begged her father not to harm the horse; then she took a firmer stand, pointing out that the accident had been her responsibility, and that it had resulted from at least some small amount of carelessness.

Don't blame the horse for the owner's mistake.

Frank ultimately relented. He would harbor nothing but disdain for Misty the rest of her days, but the love he felt for his daughter took precedence. If Lisa considered the horse to be a part of the family, then that's the way it would be.

Eventually, Mom and I were introduced to all the other mares and foals at the farm. At first nobody was too social, we were all still busy getting to know the most important part of our young lives: our mothers. Within the week, however, things had changed. All the babies smelled and

*sorted each other and began to pick up an "order." We
sorted each other into groups: those of us that are the "real
thing" . . . and everyone else. (Knowing which group you
belong to is something you just know by instinct—if
you've got "it," life can be an easy street; otherwise, you
have to work hard and hope whoever holds your future can
see you for who you are.)*

*I'll tell you right now: I am the "real thing," but I still
get chased out of the group by all the bullies. They make
me mad and I fight back. I don't need them; I've got my
mom.*

—Lisa Ann Calley
"One of a Dozen"

Things were fine for a while, until Lisa began experiencing
seizures that doctors attributed to the injury she had suffered.
The damage, they suggested, had been more extensive than
originally suspected. It was hard to tell exactly what had happened. The brain was mysterious, the neurologists explained.
Maybe the seizures would subside as Lisa grew older; maybe
not. There was no way of knowing.

Regardless of the obstacles thrown her way, Lisa remained
devoted to her horses; she rode as much as possible, but an
escalation in the number and severity of her seizures precluded
any sort of future as a competitive equestrian. In time she was
placed on Dilantin, an antiseizure medication. Although the
drug helped some, it had side effects (fatigue and drowsiness
being the most notable) and those factors, combined with the
ever-present threat of more seizures, made life a daily grind for
Lisa. Her parents worried about her passing out and falling off

a horse, or getting kicked in the head. They worried about her driving a car or even crossing a street on foot.

They worried.

"Lisa was a remarkable girl," recalled Frank Calley. "She had a hard life, but she never lost her spirit. She never stopped smiling."

Nor did she ever relinquish, or even discourage, the nurturing instinct that seemed to dominate her personality. Interesting that someone who was not physically capable of bearing children of her own was so widely regarded as having the characteristics of a great mother. She was a rescuer, the kind of person who would find a bird with a broken wing on the front lawn and nurse it back to health. She saw potential where others saw failure. She saw innate goodness where it wasn't necessarily obvious. She overlooked flaws and weaknesses and remained the eternal optimist, sometimes to her own detriment.

There was a marriage that didn't work out. He was a family friend, a nice enough man most of the time, according to Carol Calley, until he began drinking heavily and the inevitable problems and abuses began to surface. Lisa tolerated it for a while, hoped things would get better, but the cumulative weight of her seizure disorder and the daily trauma at home proved too much to bear.

As if that wasn't enough, in the early 1990s Lisa was diagnosed with cervical cancer. Her mother would always wonder about the possibility that the long-term use of Dilantin had triggered the disease, perhaps throwing a genetic switch that otherwise might always have remained in the "off" position. But what choice was there at the time? For her part, Lisa never saw the point of second-guessing. A waste of time and energy. Better to just get on with the business of life. Cut out the bad stuff, take whatever medication was available, and hope for the best.

So that's what she did, beating back the cancer with a combination of surgery (separate procedures, a week apart) and chemotherapy. Less than a year after receiving the initial diagnosis, Lisa was declared cancer-free. Not yet thirty years old, but wise enough to know for sure that life is nothing if not precious and short, she decided to make some changes. She left her husband, quit her job as a dental hygienist, and went to work in the one place where she always suspected she'd feel at home:

The racetrack.

"She wanted to get away from what was going on in her life," Carol explained. "She needed a change. It wasn't easy, and I don't recall thinking it was the best thing for her at the time, but she'd certainly earned the right to be happy."

She started where virtually everyone starts when they arrive at a track for the first time: at the very bottom of some minor league facility, in this case Finger Lakes Racetrack. Newcomers to the backstretch get the shittiest jobs, in the most literal sense of the term. They muck out stalls, change feed buckets, wash and groom the least expensive and slowest of racehorses. Lisa didn't mind. She was content to be around animals. They were less complicated than people, less demanding and generally more appreciative of the things you did for them, rewarding even the smallest of gestures with a tilt of the head or a lick on the back of the hand.

Lisa wanted nothing more out of life at that time than to

learn how to become a trainer of thoroughbred racehorses. She spent endless hours there, trying to be one of the boys in a world not known for its gender equity. She was a pretty young woman, tall and athletic, but she disguised her attractiveness with baggy jeans tugged into her work boots, blond hair hidden beneath a hooded sweatshirt. She fought against her natural inclination to smile and talk, and to be friendly with everyone who crossed her path. It wasn't easy.

"She was an extraordinary person," said John Tebbutt, the Finger Lakes trainer who got to know Lisa shortly after she arrived on the backstretch. "She worked in the same barn as I did. I had horses on one side and she went to work for a trainer on the other side. I liked her right from the start. She was kind to the horses, had a sweet personality, and she worked her butt off."

Not long after we came inside, the humans made their way into each stall to get acquainted with their new pupils. I wasn't up to anyone fussing with me, so I kicked at the handler and was left alone. A short while later, a man came in. We wrestled, he won, and I spent the afternoon tied in the corner. The other horses accepted the humans and went along with the program of being saddled and bridled, then introduced to a rider and so on and so forth.

I, however, had something ingrained in me—by pedigree, perhaps—that told me not to trust humans.

—Lisa Ann Calley
"One of a Dozen"

Chapter Three

The boy stood on the side of the highway, watching the trucks and cars roll by, unsure of everything, certain of nothing, except that he had to get away, put as much distance as possible between himself and the son of a bitch who had taken hold of his family. You don't break a bottle over your stepfather's head and expect him to welcome you back with open arms. Some things can't be corrected or forgiven. Some things you don't want to correct. But there are limited options for a fifteen-year-old boy, especially one who looks to be about twelve and has only a few dollars in his pocket. He would rely on the generosity of strangers simply because there was no other choice; and anyway, could they hurt him any more than he'd been hurt in his own home?

But where would he go?

There was only one reasonable plan, it seemed. He would

head south to California, where his sister would be happy to put him up for a while, until he got a handle on things. She would sympathize, right? She didn't like the new guy, either, never understood what their mother saw in him, or why she had followed him all over the country. She'd find out that Timmy had whacked him over the head with a milk bottle and give the kid a high five. With Cheryl, at least, he'd have a roof over his head and a place to sleep—a place where no one would get all liquored up and then berate him and tell him he was worthless and knock him around simply for having the temerity to stand up for himself.

A few days later, the boy showed up on the doorstep of his big sister's apartment. She gave him a hug, welcomed him in, gave him something to eat, and the two of them commiserated about the direction their lives had taken. At the time, Cheryl wanted nothing more than to help her little brother, but reality has a way of interfering with good intentions. The truth of the matter was this: Cheryl was in no position, financially or emotionally, to serve as a surrogate parent to Tim. Practically speaking, their living arrangement was doomed from the outset.

"Keep in mind, he's fifteen years old, and I'm only twenty-one," Cheryl recalled. "I've already got two kids of my own, and no one to help me raise them. I'm all alone in California, I don't really even know anyone, and I've got hardly any money. I'm an East Coast girl who only came out west because my mother invited me, and now she's gone. I'm in a strange world with two little kids, trying to take care of them and support them . . . and all of a sudden along comes my brother Timmy."

Cheryl laughed.

"It didn't last very long at all. Mainly because he was driving me crazy."

At some point—a few weeks, maybe a month, according to Tim—brother and sister agreed that Tim would have to find another place to live. Since he was too young to get a real job and had no friends or family in the area, Tim decided he had only one viable option:

He would track down his father.

"Sounds crazy, I know," Tim said. "But what else was I going to do? I knew my dad was somewhere in New England, still riding, or at least working at a track somewhere. He didn't know how to do anything else. How hard could it be to find him? There aren't that many racetracks in New England. I figured I'd start at Suffolk Downs and work my way north until he turned up. I had family back there anyway. My uncle worked at Suffolk, and I had a grandfather who was working at a restaurant in Rhode Island, or so I heard. It's not like I had a real plan or anything. I just figured my father would be somewhere in New England, so I took a shot."

It took him nearly a week to cross the country, the first of a couple hundred such trips he would make in his lifetime, almost all by car or thumb. Times were different then, of course. This was 1970, which was really just an extension of the sixties, with its reassuring if somewhat naive notion of peace, love, and understanding, when you couldn't drive more than a few miles without coming across a hitchhiker, seemingly with his entire life strapped to his back. There is a tendency to romanticize the past; even in the sixties, not everyone found the open road to be a hospitable place, and not every driver felt secure enough to open his doors to each smiling, pony-tailed, paisley-shirted hitchhiker he came across. But the truth is, it was a more innocent time, and the scraggly little teen who walked out onto a dusty road had no problem catching a ride. And not once in the ensuing days did anyone try to hurt him, steal from him (not that he had much worth taking), or otherwise take advantage of him.

Maybe there was some Dickensian thing about the kid that made people want to help him. Or, perhaps, once aboard they got to know him a little, caught that whiff of survival that followed him, and thought better of trying to mess him up. Something about the kid made it clear that he wouldn't go down without a fight. Regardless, Tim Snyder recalls the trip nostalgically.

"Didn't have a problem," he said. "Slept in cars, trucks. Didn't meet a bad person."

Depends on how you identify the term, of course. There was the truck driver hauling a crane, taking back roads and side roads and roads that were barely roads at all in an attempt to beat the scales and save some money. The guy gave Tim some food, told great stories, and advised him that if they ever got pulled over, the kid should jump out of the truck and run as fast as he could. So Timmy kept his suitcase by his side, and when the inevitable happened, somewhere in the upper Midwest, he bailed before the truck even came to a complete stop.

Timmy hid in the woods for a little while, waited for the flashing lights to recede in the distance, then stuck out his thumb and quickly landed another ride. The last one was a trucker who carried the kid more than five hundred miles, all the way to Boston. Dropped him off on the side of the road in Chelsea, only a few miles from Suffolk Downs. Timmy had seventy-five dollars in his wallet, about half of that earned along the way, while loading and unloading gear for two guys who drove a truck for Allied Van Lines.

He walked from Chelsea to Revere, his destination a local pub that he vaguely recalled from his childhood. Tim had gotten to know the place through his father, who would sometimes take the boy with him when he visited the local watering holes where jockeys and backstretch workers congregated.

"But it wasn't just a bar," Tim noted. "It was an underground gambling kind of place, with a back room where you could play the slots, cards, shoot pool. All kinds of stuff."

The kid wasn't even sure the bar was still there, or that ownership hadn't changed hands. He simply remembered that his father was a regular and figured the old man was probably still a drinker and that it would be a good place to start.

He was right.

The kid walked into the dim, smoky bar, leaving daylight behind, and told everyone who he was: Timmy Snyder . . . Warren Snyder's boy.

"Anybody seen my old man?"

Of course they had. Everyone knew Warren Snyder. Hell, everyone knows everyone at the racetrack. Within a matter of minutes the kid knew exactly where and when to find his father. He was at Suffolk Downs, working as a hotwalker and groom for a trainer named J. J. Kelly. Warren had stopped

riding competitively by this time, his career cut short by injuries and laziness and a pathologically self-destructive nature.

"He wasn't a jockey by that point," Tim said matter-of-
factly. "He was pretty much just a drinker."

Fifteen-year-old kids weren't allowed on the grounds of
Suffolk Downs, or most any other racetrack in those days—at
least not if they weren't accompanied by an adult. Tim Snyder was hardly dissuaded, though; what are a few track cops
and a locked gate after you've run away from an abusive stepdad and hitchhiked three thousand miles on your own? Nothing more than a minor annoyance. The kid found a quiet spot
on the backstretch, largely ignored by racetrack security, scaled
a six-foot chain-link fence, and dropped to the other side. Then
he let instinct take over. Timmy hadn't been to Suffolk Downs
in at least five years, hadn't seen his father in more than three
years. But he knew right where to look.

"I went to the backstretch kitchen area and asked around,
what barn he was in, what room . . . that sort of thing. He was
staying on the backside, in these little bungalows they have
for track workers who can't afford anything better. Kinda
shitty. I figured that's where he'd be. Everybody knew him
because he was a pool player and a drinker. This was mid-
afternoon, when the races were just about over. Maybe like
the eighth or ninth race. I asked someone on the backstretch
where he was, and they pointed out his room to me. Back at
that time they had trailers, all lined up at the top of the stretch.
Everyone I'd talked to that day warned me that he wasn't doing well, that he was basically drunk all the time. I didn't care.
I wanted to see him."

Prepared for the worst, Timmy knocked on the door. A voice barked back at him.

"Who is it?"

The boy opened the door without answering, and walked into the room. There, not ten feet away, was Warren Snyder. Timmy smiled at him.

"Hey, Dad. How are you?"

The man stood up slowly, shambled over to greet his son. They embraced wordlessly for a few moments. Then they just stared at each other. Later, Tim would explain that his father seemed happy, or maybe just shocked.

"I know he was drunk," Tim said. "I could smell it on him. But it felt like he shook it off and sobered up real fast. We stayed in the trailer for only a little while, and then he wanted to take me out, introduce me to everyone. I guess he was trying to show me off."

Most of the day would pass before the father asked the son how the hell he had found him, and where he had come from. A fifteen-year-old boy hitchhiking all the way across the country? To reunite with his father?

Damn!

How could Warren Snyder not be impressed? Even through an alcoholic haze, his heart swelled.

But there were limits to what the guy could handle. He'd had virtually no contact with his wife or kids since the day he'd headed north and left the family behind in Florida. When Timmy tried to tell his father about the man who had taken his place, and how they'd come to blows that night in Washington, and that the kid had basically run away from home to avoid getting his ass kicked (or worse), and that his sister was in Southern California, raising two children on her own, and that the whole family had basically been blown to bits . . . well, that was almost more than Warren could bear. As Tim told the story, the man's eyes welled with tears; he shook his head.

"Please," he said. "Stop."

The kid got a tack room at Suffolk Downs and hung out with the old man for the remainder of the summer meet, and into the fall meet. The months passed quickly, the two of them reconnecting with surprising ease. Warren showed his son around the track, introduced him to a broad range of potential employers who sometimes gave the boy work and tossed him a few dollars off the books. Tim had come to Boston out of desperation more than anything else, with few expectations beyond finding a safe place to sleep at night; he was pleasantly surprised to discover that his father, while clearly having fallen to the lower region of the racetrack world, was apparently not beyond redemption. Warren liked having his son around the track, seemed proud of the boy for having made his way across the country. Probably, although it was left unspoken, he admired the kid for cracking his stepfather across the skull.

That's my boy!

Most important, Warren Snyder was sufficiently motivated by the prospect of renewed fatherhood that he set the bottle aside and tried to lead a generally sober life.

In the fall, father and son drove together to Aiken, South Carolina, home of the venerable Aiken Training Center.

"He was going to teach me how to gallop horses," Tim remembered. "That was the plan—my father and his buddies were going to make a rider out of me."

At Aiken, Tim would learn the basics of the backstretch (although much of it he already knew from firsthand experience). He would walk hots, muck out stalls, even hold horses for the blacksmiths while they shod the frequently agitated animals. Bottom-of-the-barrel jobs, just like every other neophyte. It was a sound strategy, one that showed respect for racetrack tradition and conventions. But Tim's entry into this world did not go smoothly.

"By this point my dad had started drinking pretty heavily again," Tim said. "So the first place he hit when we got to Aiken was a bar downtown where all the jump riders hung out. These guys were nut jobs—plates in their heads, a hundred broken bones, hooked on painkillers, totally whacked out. Hell, all steeplechase riders are crazy, but back then it was really a different world. Today the steeplechasers are mostly young English kids from good backgrounds, and it's a lot safer than it used to be. These guys were mostly jocks who'd gotten too big, and so they became jumpers. Weight restrictions are a lot more relaxed. But, shit . . . you gotta be a little off to be a steeplechaser, because you know you're going down eventually."

Timmy didn't care at the time, and in fact was somewhat in awe of the twisted, swaggering jumpers, with their prodigious appetites for partying and their capacity for pain. Anyway, his father was a rider and so Tim wanted to learn to ride, as well. Didn't matter what kind of horse or what type of race. Eventually he would become a jock, but his body would rebel against the notion. He was simply too big, and no amount of running or puking or cocaine was going to make him small enough to be a viable jockey. The kid's instincts were essentially correct, though: if he learned how to gallop horses, and to do just about any job on the backstretch, maybe he could support himself.

"It wasn't like I had a ton of options," Tim said. "I was fifteen years old, with no education and no money. Hey, I'm educated as far as horses. The knowledge I have you couldn't find in a book. I know kids today who go to school, pay eighteen thousand dollars to learn about horses, and they come out with nothing. I worked for a lot of people—good trainers, bad trainers, good riders, bad riders—and I got something from all of them. It's the experience you need, not just reading about it. People kept telling me I was a natural with horses; I just figured there had to be a way to make some money at it."

Once in South Carolina, it didn't take Warren long to fall completely off the wagon. He'd been hanging on by his fingertips for a while, anyway, and that first day in the bar, tossing back shots and sharing war stories with the steeplechasers and other old-time racetrack buddies, loosened his grip for good. They had come to Aiken in search of Bill Hicks, a prominent horseman and a fixture at the training center. When Hicks walked into the bar, Warren drunkenly introduced him to Timmy, slurring his words so badly that the boy was embarrassed to be in his presence. It was clear that Hicks knew Warren and likely had seen this performance before. He seemed unfazed.

"Bill sort of ran the whole town back then," Tim observed. "He gave my father a place to stay right there on the grounds of the training center, and he went right to work breezing horses. I ended up with a bunch of different jobs, and when I wasn't working the jump riders would teach me how to gallop horses. I had some money in my pocket and I was learning the ropes. It was okay. The thing is, every weekend my dad would end up in the bars with everyone else, drinking and carrying on until they had to carry him out of the place."

Timmy was amazed by his father's ability to bounce back, to get up with the sun and hop on the back of a thoroughbred, and guide the animal safely around the track despite suffering from a blinding hangover. How he didn't kill himself or wreck one of the horses was a mystery if not a miracle.

The drinking and subsequent disagreements grew tiresome, and after about a month Timmy chose to hit the road again—this time on his own. He wasn't old enough to drive legally, didn't have a license or insurance . . . but he had a functioning car, courtesy of an uncle, and soon found himself behind the wheel, heading south.

Tim wound up at another training center in Delray Beach, Florida, where he mined old racetrack connections, looking up some people who had gotten to know his father through the years. In fairly short order the kid had an apartment and the means to pay for it. He was not yet sixteen years old.

"It was a good spot for me," Tim said. "I had my own bungalow, and I broke yearlings and swam horses. I started out working older horses that already knew how to gallop, then started breaking yearlings, kind of mixed it all up. Spent a couple years there, got my galloping license, then went to work at Tropical Park in Florida, working for a Cuban guy from Chicago, galloping horses, making maybe a hundred twenty-five dollars a week. This was the early 1970s, so it wasn't bad money for the time, especially for a seventeen-year-old kid."

Life was an adventure, and Tim learned early in the process to avoid getting too attached to anyone he might come across. You can't be ready to drop everything and move if you have friends and family, or if you care about anyone too deeply. Better to travel light.

People came and went.

There was, for example, the businessman from Hallandale Beach who hired Tim to gallop his horses in the morning, and to work at his restaurant in the evening. Tim would restock the bar and vending machines, vacuum floors, mop up, then meet the owner at the track the next morning. They got to know each other, and if they weren't quite friends, neither were they merely employer and employee. Tim felt like the man cared about him, wanted to help the kid who had no family to speak of. Then, one morning after a workout, Tim jumped off the horse, handed the reins to the owner, and the two began to talk.

"All of a sudden his eyes rolled into his head," Tim remembered. "He just fell backward and died, right there on the spot."

Tim stopped as he told this story, then gathered his thoughts before continuing.

"I was totally on my own by this point. I had no contact with my family at all. My dad was up in South Carolina, my mom was out West somewhere. I didn't keep in touch with my brothers or sisters. But I made friends, or at least I got to know people. I learned to take everything one day at a time. It's like training horses—you can't plan much of anything. I mean, you can try, but the plan always gets wrecked and you have to make changes and adjust. And life is about the same way. One day you're up, the next day you're down. And sometimes you stay down for a while."

In Florida Tim reunited with a childhood friend named Dale Thirtyacre. A couple years older than Tim, and of Cherokee heritage, Dale had gotten to know Tim when they were boys, and their fathers had been jockeys together on the Southern circuit. Dale had even lived with Tim's family one summer when the Florida tracks closed for the season and the racing action shifted north.

"I lost track of Timmy for a while," Dale said. "He was going through some tough times with his stepdad, and then the family moved away, and we didn't see each other for a few years. But he had a lot of determination, and I wasn't surprised to hear that he'd run off on his own, or that he'd been hitchhiking around the country. He was an amazing kid."

As they had been as boys, Dale and Tim became virtually inseparable, first while working in South Florida, and later on a series of cross-country adventures, including one that occurred in the fall of 1972, shortly after Tropical Park went out of business. The two young men were offered an opportunity to accompany a horse van transporting roughly a dozen head of stock from Florida to Arlington Park race-track in Chicago, where, upon arrival, jobs would be waiting. They would each wear multiple hats: exercise rider, groom, stable hand. In return, each young man would receive a salary of three hundred fifty dollars.

"More money than I'd ever seen," observed Dale Thirty-acre. "A good, steady job."

Along the way, though, the two encountered tragedy on a Grand Guignol scale.

"Transporting horses is crazy work," Tim noted many years later. "The driver had already made several long trips before he picked us up, so he was probably exhausted, popping bennies or whatever they did back then to stay awake for thirty hours straight. It was totally common and pretty much unregulated. That's the way you moved horses."

You also moved horses by making sure they had human accompaniment in the back of the van. This was Tim Snyder's job: to sit in a lounge chair and generally just keep an eye on things; to feed and water the animals, make sure they remained calm, did not overheat, or otherwise experience any duress that was worth reporting. The van was basically a stable on wheels, with individual stand-up stalls for each animal. The horses were grouped in rows of three, in alternating positions: the first three with heads facing in one direction, the next three with heads facing in the opposite direction. Each animal was secured in place by chains that stretched from the edge of the stall to the horse's bridle. As the van prepared to pull away, Tim checked the animals one more time, then took his seat in the back of the van, opened up a newspaper, and tried to relax. Driving a car behind the van was Dale Thirtyacre.

As such trips usually are, this one was uneventful for the first several hundred miles, until the van crossed the Tennessee-Kentucky border, while traveling on the Kentucky turnpike, and came upon an accident that had snarled traffic for some distance.

"I don't know if he didn't see it, or if he was slow to react, or what happened," recalled Dale Thirtyacre, "but the driver of the van plowed right into the back of a semi, and the horse van buckled sideways. At first, it didn't look that bad. Not as bad as it was, anyway."

While Dale looked on, all hell was breaking loose inside the van—animals being torn loose from their chains and tossed against the walls, and crashing into one another. Some were killed instantly, their spines snapped by the impact. Others had their throats slit by the chains. Still others survived the initial crash, only to panic and trample each other.

And in the middle of it all was Tim Snyder.

"I never lost consciousness," Tim said. "I didn't even really get hurt. Don't ask me how. When we got hit my lounge chair folded up and I was stuck inside. Then the horses started falling around me, crying and wailing and trying to get out. I ended up on the floor of the van, with a horse right on top of me, kind of half hanging by the chain around its neck. There was blood everywhere and the doors of the van were blown right off."

Dale Thirtyacre ran from his car to the back of the van. Along with the driver and several bystanders, they rushed into the stable area and began looking for Tim, pushing through the carnage and the stink.

"I figured he was dead," said Dale. "I mean . . . it was horrible. There was just no way he could have survived."

Except he did. The horse that had fallen on Tim had somehow not crushed him, and the animal's body had served as a shield from the impact of the collision, and from the careening horses that followed. Tim was pulled from the wreckage, dazed and covered in gore, but without a scratch on him.

"I think he was in shock," Dale observed. "I was, too."

Cops and paramedics were soon on the scene, along with a veterinarian and a new van to transport the handful of surviving horses for the remainder of the trip. According to Snyder, the trainer of the fatally injured horses later tried to sue the van company in order to help recoup losses from the accident. He also tried to recruit the van's passenger in his efforts.

"I'm pretty sure he had borrowed money from the mob, and he was in big trouble," Tim said. "He needed those horses to pay off his debts. In the end he didn't get much from the van company, so he tried to get me to say that I was injured, so that he'd have a better lawsuit."

Tim thought about going along with the trainer, until one day he ran into a hard-looking man on the shedrow.

"I heard your back's bothering you," the man said.

Tim shrugged, not sure what to make of him. He knew the guy was not a regular on the backstretch. "Maybe a little."

The man smiled.

"Yeah? Well, tomorrow it might hurt a lot more."

Tim said nothing in response, but he got the message. Loud and clear. He packed his bags and left Arlington Park that night.

And never went back.

Dale's 1969 Plymouth Roadrunner 383 took them from Chicago to Southern California, where the two boys picked up work for the trainer Richard Mulhall at Del Mar Racetrack. They were young and tireless, had good hands and an easy way with horses, could gallop just about anything, and were sufficiently connected in the backstretch world, so it wasn't hard for them to find jobs.

There wasn't much not to like about Del Mar—with its seaside setting and cool ocean breezes, it remains even today widely regarded as one of the world's most breathtaking tracks. Like Saratoga, there was a brevity to the summer meeting that infused the entire season with a sense of urgency. The top trainers and riders and owners descended on the place each summer, traveling down the Pacific Coast Highway from Santa Anita to the outskirts of San Diego, for something that amounted to a hardworking vacation.

Timmy and Dale burned the candle at both ends, rising at five each morning; sometimes rising wasn't even necessary, for they'd never gone to sleep.

"For a long time I hated alcohol, because of my dad," Tim said. "I had seen what it did to people and wanted no part of it. I didn't drink at all until I was close to twenty years old, and then I started hitting it pretty hard. I thought it was cool, and

I liked the way it felt—except for the hangovers, of course. Must be in my blood, because I got into the habit pretty quickly. That turned out to be a mistake. I found after a while that when I drink, the shades go down. I black out, don't remember a thing. That's bad; it's dangerous."

For a while, though, when he was young and healthy, the drinking caused only minor inconveniences and embarrassment. The "truth serum," as his father-in-law would later call it, was a social lubricant that made it easy for him to talk with people, to gain their confidence and trust. Timmy could be temperamental and distant, perfectly understandable given his background and upbringing, but give him a couple drinks and he'd tell you his life story. And he'd listen to yours, which was even more important if you were seeking companionship from a young woman you'd just met.

"Timmy generally always had women around him," noted Cheryl Hall. "In fact, he had a string of nice, pretty girlfriends over the years. Some of them became my friends, and remain my friends even today. These weren't one-night stands. These were smart, attractive women from good families. And they usually had money; and ad people who own horses tend to have money. They met Tim through the horse racing industry. I'd say to him, 'Timmy, how do you get these ladies?' And he'd say, 'Cheryl, women love horses. It's a given.' But I don't mean to imply that he was a womanizer, or that he flitted from flower to flower. He didn't. For as long as each relationship lasted, he would treat them well and with respect. That was his MO."

Timmy and Dale took regular trips across the border to party in Tijuana, where ten bucks would get you a night's worth of drinking, a big meal, and maybe even a pretty girl on your arm. During one such visit, the timing chain on the Roadrunner snapped, leaving the boys stranded for nearly three weeks while they waited for a local repair shop to acquire parts and get the job done. They passed the time hanging out at the beach and the local racetrack, drinking tequila and beer, and baking in the sun. By the time the car was repaired, they were practically broke and had no job prospects, since the Del Mar meeting had come to a close. They drove back into California, meandering through the southern reaches of the Inland Empire, eventually landing near Temecula, which at the time was less developed and home to a number of horse farms. They worked as ranch hands for a while before hopping into the Plymouth and driving back across the country to Florida.

Within a year, though, Tim had hit the road again. Alone.

"Timmy kind of has a way of disappearing on you," Dale Thirtyacre said. "We were like brothers, the best of friends. And then one day he was just . . . gone."

It was not the first time that Tim had shown up unannounced at his sister's door, and it would not be the last.

He had tracked her to Encinitas, a tony suburb of San Diego not far from Del Mar. Funny, Tim thought. The whole time he'd been working at the track, his sister had been just a few miles away, and he hadn't even known it. Back then, though, he wasn't really interested in finding her; now he was. He couldn't explain it, really.

"I was just hungry to find her," Tim said. "I started

thinking about my family, trying to locate them, and Cheryl was the only one I could find. I didn't even call ahead, just marched up to the front door, rang the bell, and waited for her to answer."

Cheryl was stunned when she saw her brother. She stood speechless, letting the pages of the mental calendar fall away as she hugged him.

"I'm home," he said. "Hope you don't mind."

Cheryl had built a life of her own. Like Tim, she had no idea what had become of her parents, although she did keep in touch with her two other younger brothers. Cheryl was industrious and not prone to self-pity. With two kids, she couldn't afford to indulge any wanderlust that might have been handed down from her parents (Tim had certainly inherited some of that). Instead she tried to provide a stable household for her family. In addition to her day job, she bought an ice cream truck and worked nights and weekends driving around the neighborhood, setting up shop near baseball fields and soccer pitches and playgrounds. She socked enough money to buy her own house, in the hope of giving her kids something she did not have while growing up: a sense of place; a home.

For a while it became Tim's home, as well.

"My sister is a very generous person," Tim said. "She used to give away almost as much ice cream as she sold. She didn't expect to have little brother move in, but she didn't complain. We shared expenses and I helped out as best I could."

Tim worked mostly at private training centers, galloping horses and breaking yearlings, which was an art unto itself.

"Nothing quite like catching them from scratch, when they haven't been handled at all," Tim said. "And they do it a lot different out there in the West. The horses are pretty wild; you gotta be careful. You have to know what you're doing, show them the right amount of respect, but also let them know you're in control. I'd tack them, drive them, jib rope them, get all the bucks out of them in the bullpen, in deep sand. Sometimes I'd try to overpower them, sometimes I'd try to befriend them. They're all different. Some will nuzzle right up to you; others will stomp around and try to kick the shit out of you."

Tim would know, having suffered more injuries over the years than he can recount: broken legs, nose, pelvis, separated shoulder, just to name a few.

"It's part of the game," he said. "You work with horses for a living, you're going to get busted up every once in a while."

He was living in Ocala, Florida, in the fall of 1977, breaking yearlings for a handful of private clients, when he found out that his mother had died. The news came one afternoon, shortly after Tim, using a heavy dose of tough love, had finished breaking a colt that had seemed all but unbreakable. He was standing with the horse, stroking its forehead, when the owner's son approached the stable.

"Hey, Tim," he said. "Mom wants to see you up at the house."

Tim nodded, tried to conceal his anxiety.

Here we go . . . I'm gonna lose my job over this damn horse.

They walked in silence. Inside the house, the woman greeted Tim warmly. She invited him to sit down, opened up a bottle of scotch, and poured them each a drink. By this point Tim realized that the meeting had nothing to do with the way he had handled or mishandled any of the woman's horses.

"I have something to tell you," she said.

Tim drained his glass. He didn't often drink scotch, not the good kind, anyway, and he wasn't about to let it go to waste, regardless of the circumstances.

"All right," he said. "Go ahead."

The woman nodded.

"You mother has passed away."

Tim said nothing, just sat there silently fumbling with his empty glass. Whatever he was supposed to feel—grief, anger, sadness—wasn't there.

"Do you understand, Tim?" the woman asked.

He nodded. "Where did it happen?"

"Houston," the woman said. "The funeral is tomorrow. I bought you a plane ticket."

Tim thanked the woman, returned to his apartment, and packed some clothes for the trip.

In Houston Tim was reunited with his siblings, as well as the stepfather he hadn't seen since the day he'd busted a milk bottle over the man's head some seven years earlier.

"They all treated me like I was back from the dead," Tim remembered. "At first I was kind of disappointed they hadn't tried to contact me when they found out Mom was sick, but I was invisible, really, and it turned out my mom didn't want any of us to see her that way. She and my stepfather had been living pretty well, too, until her health went bad. She had opened up a restaurant and bar in Corpus Christi, owned a couple liquor stores and two or three Laundromats. Even bought a church one time. My mom could touch anything and it would turn to gold; she could step in shit and have it turn to gold. Of course, I didn't know any of this until she died, and the FBI tracked me down in Florida."

He wasn't the only one who had lost touch with Virginia Snyder. In fact, she had become a ghost to her entire family.

"I kept the same number for four years, hoping she would call," said Cheryl Hall. "But she never did. She was sick in the hospital for more than a year and didn't call. She didn't want to see us or speak to us, and supposedly told everyone around her, 'Don't call my family until I'm gone.'

"But it wasn't that she didn't love us. It's just that through the years, she'd established a condition of . . . leaving things . . . and never looking back. Whether it was a houseful of furniture or friends and relatives. Whatever. I remember she hocked her earrings once. She had a beautiful diamond ring; hocked that, too. I asked her about them once, and she just sort of laughed and waved her hand. 'Oh, I was glad to see them go.' That was the life she and my father led: feast or famine. Steak one day, canned soup the next. That's the racetrack life. You don't get too attached to things."

Tim never saw his stepfather again. They were cordial at the funeral, and afterward went their separate ways. According to Tim and Cheryl, he sold off their mother's various business interests and moved to Puerto Rico.

"He was kind of a cold-hearted bastard," Tim said matter-of-factly. "I never cared for him at all, never trusted him. He was a bad guy, far as I'm concerned. Only out for himself. I still don't know what my mother saw in him."

What she saw, Cheryl believes, was an escape from the racetrack life. Ironically, though, she swapped one insecure existence for another, and one unreliable partner for another.

"In the end, he was just as abusive and drunk as my father was," Cheryl observed. "And my mother died an alcoholic. I don't think she drank much at all until she was in her twenties, but then I guess over time she just felt like, If you can't beat 'em, join 'em. In many ways she was a wonderful woman, but that's the truth of the situation."

Horse sense Tim inherited from his father; the running and leaving, the inability to stay in one place for any length of time, or to commit fully to a job or a person or a lifestyle? That trait could be found on both sides of the family tree.

Tim bounced all over the continent in the 1980s—from California to Florida, from New England to Canada, before finally settling in Central New York, where he found consistent backstretch work for the trainer Bill Strange. It was Strange who encouraged Tim to take the test required to become a licensed trainer himself, which he did in 1986.

By the end of the decade he had fathered two children. The first, a daughter named Sierra, was born in California in 1980. Tim had split with the girl's mother before she was born, and insists he did not even know at the time that the woman was pregnant. Sierra's family lived not far from Cheryl, and through his sister Tim was able to maintain a tenuous long-distance relationship with Sierra. They met for the first time when the little girl was two years old, when Tim went to California for a visit.

"Finding out I had a daughter blew me away," he said. "My sister is the one who actually has kept us together. She developed a relationship with Sierra's family, and they see each other practically every week. It's been a little challenging. There was another guy involved; he ended up raising my daughter, and I don't think he really ever wanted me involved. I can't blame him, and I've got no problem with him. He and Sierra's mom have done a beautiful job with her. She's a great girl."

From a different relationship, Tim also has a son several years younger than Sierra.

"We don't have any contact," he said matter-of-factly. "His mother was a gold digger, been married five or six times. Last I heard she was married to a multimillionaire."

Tim shrugged.

"I'm not impressed by money. I've been around some people with a lot of it. I trained horses for them, I worked for them. I've had bosses who've lied and cheated. I've worked for people who've embezzled money and gone to jail. There's a lot of bad actors in horse racing, and I've seen all types. I'm not perfect, but I try to keep myself on a fairly straight line, because when you step over that line, you can get in big trouble. I ain't saying I never stole anything, but I never stole to buy drugs or to line my pocket. I did steal to put food in my belly. I admit that. I stole to survive."

An elliptical, energetic talker and storyteller, Tim paused momentarily before circling back.

"My son? I heard he's okay. I hope so."

Chapter Four

OCALA, FLORIDA
APRIL 11, 2007

The horse that dropped that morning was one of scores foaled in 2007 at Ocala Stud, a venerable facility with a half-century record of breeding quality thoroughbred racehorses. With a training track, starting gate and more than five hundred acres of land spread out over three different farms, Ocala Stud is one of the largest and most comprehensive breeding and training operations in the United States. The farm has produced more than one hundred stakes winners, the majority of whom were also sired by Ocala stallions. In short, it is a self-contained and self-sufficient business.

There is an established and traditional blueprint for bringing racehorses from the farm to the racetrack, and Ocala Stud has long utilized a variation on this theme. Mares are bred to stallions, and the resulting offspring are put into training roughly halfway through their yearling year (at approximately one and a half years of age). Those that adequately handle the training are sold as two-year-olds, either through private transactions or at the Ocala Spring Sales. Of the approximately seventy horses foaled at Ocala in 2007, all but a few would successfully navigate this course. Whether they would actually make it to the starting line of a race was another matter altogether, for horse racing is among the most unpredictable of sports, and thoroughbreds among the most temperamental and fragile of athletes. At Ocala Stud, though, the babies typically grow up to be racehorses, or at least racehorses-in-training.

The few that wash out, for whatever reason, are simply given away.

"But that almost never happens," explained Michael O'Farrell, manager of Ocala Stud. "We sell just about every horse we raise."

So it would be for the big bay filly with the splash of white across her nose. Although of relatively modest lineage, she was an attractive girl, tall and lean, with a good deal of spirit. If there are no complications in the birthing process, and no obvious physical abnormalities immediately apparent, there isn't much you can tell about the aspirations of a newborn foal. There is no way to measure heart and competitive desire; no way to tell whether she's hit the genetic lottery, drawing on all that is quick and efficient in her gene pool and casting aside all that might cause her to weaken or quit.

Those answers come later.

In the case of the bay foal, cautious optimism seemed the most prudent course of action. She was the product of a union between the mare Ennuhway, a daughter of Ocala Stud stallion Notebook, and Drewman, also an Ocala Stud stallion. Dig back a few generations and you could find some significant racing and breeding talent in the foal's lineage: the prodigious stud Mr. Prospector and Hall of Fame competitor Dr. Fager on the sire's side; Bold Ruler (sire of Secretariat) on the distaff side. But neither Ennuhway nor Drewman had been particularly distinguished, either at the track or in the breeding shed, leaving the unnamed filly with a pedigree of questionable value.

Yet there was no denying the horse's physical stature—her clean lines and skeletal structure. Breeding is as much about hope and luck as it is science. You throw all that DNA into a blender and hit the switch, and then you stand back and let nature take its course. There is no shortage of tantalizing success stories, tales of plodding nags who inexplicably foal champions; conversely, of course, there are plenty of stories about magnificent competitors who were flaccid on the farm, or whose progeny failed to live up to expectations. Secretariat was the most notable example, although his legacy was not nearly as diminished as some would believe; it was more a matter of inevitable disappointment given the extraordinary standard to which his offspring were held.

Simply put: you never know how things are going to turn out.

Michael O'Farrell took one look at the brand-new filly and figured she'd gotten the best that Drewman and Ennuhway had to offer. Indeed, O'Farrell was sufficiently optimistic of the foal's future that he paid the five-hundred-dollar nominating fee for the Breeders Cup. While that certainly couldn't be considered a large sum of money in the world of horse

racing, it did speak to the foal's potential and the optimism of
her owners; it's worth noting, for example, that O'Farrell was
not in the habit of nominating every horse foaled at the farm.
Some simply did a better job of passing the test. That, apparently, was the case with the daughter of Drewman and Ennuhway.

She would be a runner.

Like every healthy horse foaled at Ocala, the filly went
into training a few months after her first birthday, and before
long it became apparent that in this case, at least, looks were
deceptive. Although big and strong, and presenting the appearance of a competitive racehorse, she did not tolerate workouts well and seemed less inclined to run than the rest of her
class. Whether this was some innate characteristic of her personality, or the result of a physiological problem was difficult
to ascertain. There were no obvious injuries or structural
abnormalities. She was just . . . slow.

O'Farrell had lost any hope that the filly might one day
run in the Breeders Cup; in fact, he had begun to doubt whether
she would ever stand in a starting gate—anywhere. As the
deadline grew near for the Ocala Breeders Company Spring
Sale in April 2009, O'Farrell was forced to make a decision.

"We had her entered in the sale here at Ocala, and she
wasn't coming up to it the way we would have liked," O'Farrell
recalled. "We normally breeze our horses a quarter mile prior
to the sales, and she would have been at the bottom of the list
of horses that we had as far as ability—at least in terms of
what she had shown."

In addition to apparently lacking the requisite talent to
be a racehorse, the filly began having trouble recovering

from workouts, which only served to further discourage her handlers.

"She had a setback shortly before the sales," O'Farrell said. "We call it 'tying up,' which basically means the muscles tighten when they exert too much energy. It's not a big issue, most of the time. It's part of training horses. They're usually over it within twenty-four hours, but it's best if you give them some time off afterward, especially when they're so young. With this horse, though, it happened right before the sales, so we were between a rock and a hard place. So we took her out of the sale, sent her back to the farm, turned her out for two or three weeks to let her get over it, and then put her back in training."

Although seemingly healthy, the filly was no more inclined to run than she'd been before her recuperation. Her continued struggles, coupled with a nasty downturn in the economy, led O'Farrell to rethink his plans for the horse.

"This was right around the time the housing bubble burst, the economy had gone to hell, and horse sales had dropped like 30 to 40 percent," O'Farrell said. "So we were stuck with a horse that did not seem to have any speed, and was unlikely to get much quicker. She came out of a stallion that was not particularly successful—in fact, you would pretty much consider him to be unsuccessful—and the mare had not produced a whole lot at the time, either. The filly had never shown a lot of ability, even when she was healthy."

O'Farrell, a soft-spoken man who has been around the game long enough to know that there is no such thing as a sure thing, paused momentarily, then laughed quietly under his breath.

"I just figured it was best to get rid of her."

They could have worked with her a little longer, given her a chance to demonstrate some potential in time for the next sale, in June 2009, but it hardly seemed worth the effort. No sense throwing good money after bad. O'Farrell did not even think the horse would be worth the trouble of a private transaction. Better to just hand her off to someone who specialized in this sort of thing, with no money involved.

"One of my trainers, George Burrows, is very good friends with a fellow here in Ocala who deals in . . . I won't call them *cheap* horses; I would call them inexpensive horses," O'Farrell said. "So we gave the filly to him. And that's the last I ever saw of her."

Six weeks later, John Shaw, the horse broker on the receiving end of that transaction, put in a call to Burrows, just to let him know how things were going. Shaw could only complain so much, since the filly hadn't cost him a dime, aside from the usual expenses associated with the care and feeding of a racehorse. But, Jesus, what on Earth had he gotten himself into?

"That filly you gave me?" he told Burrows. "Gotta be the slowest horse I have ever seen."

Chapter Five

APRIL 1993

If this had been Hollywood and it had happened in a romantic comedy, they would have called it "meeting cute." But since this was Farmington, New York, some twenty-five miles outside of Rochester, on the backstretch of Finger Lakes Racetrack, the introduction provoked the sort of salty language one might expect of a near fatality.

At the time, Tim Snyder was working as an assistant for Bill Strange, a trainer who ran one of the largest and most successful barns at Finger Lakes. Granted, Finger Lakes was a second-tier facility, where the stock on race days would rarely be confused with the elite thoroughbreds you'd see downstate at Belmont or at Saratoga in the summertime. There is a pecking order in horse racing, as there is in any other sport, and Finger Lakes was a couple rungs below the top. Within that world, though, Bill Strange was one of the best—among the leading trainers in North America, actually, in terms of winning percentage—and Tim Snyder was his right-hand man, an assistant who could be counted on to handle just about any job that was asked of him. Strange typically kept twenty-five to thirty horses in his barn, and Tim was involved with most of them, either as a groom, exercise rider, or hotwalker.

"Whatever Bill needed, I did it," Tim remembers. "No job was too big or too small."

Lisa Calley didn't think any job was beneath her, either, which was a good thing, given that she was new to the back-stretch and thus assigned most of the low-level tasks around the barn occupied by the trainer Eddie Babcock. Tim had seen Lisa at the track from time to time but the two had not been introduced, despite the fact that they worked in adjacent barns. Looking at Lisa, in her work boots and jeans, and a baggy sweatshirt with the hood pulled up over her head, it was hard not to think that she had no interest in small talk. She looked like a *hobo,* Tim would say years later, like a woman who did not want to be thought of as a woman, or the object of attention, but rather simply as someone capable of doing her job. Tim knew nothing of her backstory—of the failed marriage or the cancer—but he got the impression just by looking at her that she had no interest in meeting a man, or letting anyone into her life.

Fate, though, has a way of intervening in these things.

Tim was on the back of an ornery horse that morning, a bad actor that had a reputation for galloping when he wasn't supposed to gallop, and for refusing to go where he was asked to go. While guiding the rambunctious colt back to its stall, Tim suddenly found himself on an unintended joyride. As the horse raced along the shedrow, bucking and snorting, Tim shouted to everyone in his path.

"Get the hell out of the way! I can't stop!"

People scattered as the colt went by. By the time Lisa knew what was happening, it was too late. She was holding a horse of her own and now the runaway was on them, and she had nowhere to hide.

"I can still see her face," Tim said with a laugh. "She turned around and looked up at me, and she had this blank expression. Then she put her hand up, like she was going to stop the crazy horse or something, and I just kept yelling at her to move. Next thing I knew, I was sliding by her, in between her and her horse, but there wasn't enough room, and I knocked her into the wall. Pretty hard, too."

Tim rode out of the barn and across the street and then into another barn before he was finally able to convince the horse to stop. He dismounted, grabbed the horse by its bridle, gave it a good tug, delivered a few choice epithets, and led him back across the street and into the shedrow. Lisa was standing there, shaken but otherwise unharmed. Tim was immediately taken by the woman's toughness, by her spunk, but now that he was closer and could see her with the hoodie pulled back, he was also taken by something else.

"She looked so young," Tim said. "And she was so pretty."

Before guiding his horse back to its stall, Tim stopped and chatted for a while with the new girl. He asked if she was okay; she smiled, laughed it off like someone who had been around horses her entire life—which of course she had, though Tim didn't know it at the time.

For the next couple days they talked occasionally while

working. Then, one afternoon, Lisa surprised Tim by asking him a question:

"Do you like spaghetti?"

Tim said that he did like spaghetti. Very much.

"Because my grandma makes the best sauce . . . if you'd like to come over for dinner sometime."

Tim didn't know what to make of the new girl. She'd been so quiet, always kept to herself and did her work, and now here she was, inviting him to dinner just a few days after he'd nearly killed her. Was she charming . . . or crazy?

He settled on charming, accepted the invitation, and went back to work.

Lisa, it turned out, had done her homework, poking around the backstretch, inquiring about the man who had nearly run her down. She didn't have to look long or hard for information; virtually everyone at Finger Lakes knew Tim Snyder. He was a little man with a big personality, a penchant for telling stories and, to be perfectly honest, a prodigious appetite for alcohol. Everyone knew Tim was a good horseman, and most people genuinely liked him, at least in small doses. But even his best friends would sometimes grow tired of his volatility and his unpredictable nature.

"Tim is a unique guy," said John Tebbutt, who has known Snyder for nearly three decades and is, by all accounts, his closest friend. "He knows the racetrack, he can do just about anything you ask of him. He's truly an outstanding horseman. He commands respect from the animals; sometimes I think that's because he's almost as much horse as he is human. And I mean that in a good way. He bonds with them like few people I've ever known. The downside to that is that he's a high-maintenance person. He can be a loyal friend, but he's hard to get along with; he's demanding, and he can be rude. I like Tim very, very much. We go back a long way and we've been friends for an awful lot of years. But those are his characteristics. It's not his fault. It's the way he was raised and the life he led. But that's an honest appraisal of Tim, and I think he'd have to admit it."

A truncated version of that assessment was communicated by Tebbutt to Lisa Calley during the course of a normal workday. One has to be cautious, of course, when intruding upon matters of the heart, especially when they involve close friends and coworkers. Tebbutt and Snyder were not merely fellow horsemen; they were drinking buddies, as well. And while Tebbutt didn't mind closing a bar or two with Tim, he was uneasy about the prospect of recommending him as a suitor.

"I liked Lisa right from the start," Tebbutt said. "We worked on opposite sides of the same barn, so I saw her every day, and you couldn't help but be impressed by her. She was hardworking and good at her job, but the main thing was that she was so kind to the horses. She had a sweet personality, just a gentle soul. When Timmy came around and started hitting on her, I immediately told her, 'Don't get involved with him. He's a real nice guy, but keep your distance.'

"I knew too much about Timmy. He was rough around the edges, so different from Lisa. They really were an odd couple, except for the fact that they both loved horses, obviously. She was a kind, sweet little girl from a nice family in Syracuse. I tried to look out for the young girls who showed up on the backstretch. I've had a lot of them work for me over the years, and I always felt a responsibility. You run into a lot of people like Timmy—guys who were born and bred at the racetrack. It can be a rough place."

Tebbutt did his best to squelch the budding relationship; in addition to warning Lisa, he told Snyder, in no uncertain terms, to leave the girl alone. Tim's response:

"Mind your own damn business."

Years later Tebbutt would laugh and shake his head at the memory of that conversation, and of his failed efforts to keep the two apart.

"I was so surprised it developed into anything," he said. "I think Lisa was looking for something different in her life, something more exciting. She loved horses, but she also loved the racetrack world. She wanted to travel around, experience the whole thing. With Timmy, she could do that. He was an adventure. But I can't imagine her family was too happy about the whole thing, at least not in the beginning."

On that point he was correct. Like the daughter they produced, the Calleys were a generous and accepting family, but there was something about Tim Snyder that made them wary. There was the difference in their ages, for one thing. Tim was ten years older than Lisa; with a lot of hard miles on the engine, as they say, he could have passed for her father. Then, too, there was the fact that he was such a hard-core race-track lifer. Lisa had grown up around horses, too, but show jumping was a far more genteel endeavor. If she was suddenly enamored of the backstretch, with its incessant buzz of activity and its whiff of danger . . . well, her parents were less sanguine.

Lisa was twenty-seven years old, so she was hardly a

child. She had survived a broken marriage, a traumatic brain injury, and cancer. She was tougher than her appearance might have indicated. Nevertheless, some things never change. You're a mother or father from the moment your child is born. You never stop worrying and fretting. You never stop loving and caring.

"To be perfectly honest," remembered Frank Calley, "I didn't know what to make of Tim. I'd never met anyone like him."

Neither had Carol. Sitting one afternoon in the kitchen of her home outside Syracuse, looking back on that first spaghetti dinner, she could only smile.

"Compared to the way we were, the kind of people we'd known? Timmy was . . . *odd*," she said.

Sitting in the same room, just a few feet away, Tim began to laugh. "I'm odd? Thanks a lot, Carol!"

"Well, you know what I mean. We didn't know what to think. Tim used to tell such wild stories. We couldn't believe that anyone had actually lived like that. It was so different from the way we had raised our children."

Ah, yes . . . the stories. Tales of crisscrossing the country, living out of cars and camping under the stars, of supporting himself as an adult when he wasn't yet old enough to drive a car or buy a beer (legally, anyway). Stories about working for men of questionable character, men who embezzled money and went to prison, sometimes dragging family members down with them. Stories about gamblers and drug dealers and tax cheats. Stories about mobsters and movie stars: When they filmed the remake of *The Champ* at Hialeah in the late 1970s, for example, Tim was working at the track. He said he got a job galloping horses for the production and a small check for appearing as an extra in crowd scenes. Brushes with greatness and brushes with fame, some intentional, some not. There was the time in the late eighties when he was working a feisty colt at Rockingham Park, on the same late-winter day that a production crew was shooting exterior scenes for the television show *Spenser: For Hire.* The horse fought with Tim throughout the workout and bolted as they left the track, carrying his rider down a narrow road and straight toward the television crew. As Tim struggled vainly to gain control of the animal, people began screaming at him to bail out. After galloping wildly past a crowd, he pulled the horse toward a snowbank and let go of the reins, jumping off at what he guessed was a speed of thirty miles per hour.

"I just went down and rolled, must have slid about twenty feet," Tim recalled. "I burned a hole right through my boot. And the horse . . . Jesus . . . the horse went up over the snowbank and caught a foot, catapulted into a Dumpster, and broke his neck. If I hadn't got off him at the last second, I'd have been right there with him."

When things settled down and the horse's carcass was hauled away, a man in a suit approached Tim, asked if he was okay—he wasn't; a cracked vertebra would leave him limping for months—and then handed him a business card.

"He wanted to know if I'd be interested in doing some stunt work," Tim said. "I just laughed. 'Mister, I couldn't do that twice if I wanted to. But thanks, anyway.'"

The stories spilled from him effortlessly and endlessly, shaping a portrait of a racetrack Kerouak, a man always on the move, always searching for something; worried, perhaps, that if he sat still long enough, he might just die. There were stories of girlfriends who put themselves through pharmacy school by producing and trafficking synthetic cocaine; or who cooked the books for employers and wound up behind bars; of children he fathered but barely knew, or did not know at all.

"At first I wasn't sure whether to believe him," Carol said. "But then he kept telling the same stories, over and over, and always with the same details. Then I'd meet other people who knew him, and they'd say they'd heard the same stories, word for word. And then I met his sister . . . I guess some people really do live like that."

True or not—and while some of it can be verified, much of it cannot—it was enough to make your head spin. Carol wanted her daughter to be happy, though, and for whatever reason Timmy made her smile. So it wasn't long before Carol began treating him like a member of the family. Fathers, though, can be a tougher sell, and Frank withheld approval for quite some time. Whether Tim was a bullshit artist or a man who had truly lived the life he claimed to have led was of little importance to Frank. Either way, he was a man best kept at arm's length.

"My husband was harder," Carol said. "He liked Lisa's first husband; they got along well, did a lot of things together. They were friends, so it was hard for my husband when the marriage ended. And Timmy could not have been more different. My husband likes anybody, but for Lisa . . . I don't know. I just think he was cautious."

If there was one thing that Tim had in common with Lisa's first husband, according to those who knew them both well, it was a capacity for alcohol. John Tebbutt remembers

bonding with Tim the way people do when they share surroundings and circumstances and hobbies. They came to
know each other in the early 1980s, at Finger Lakes, when
both men were eking out a living on the backstretch. It wasn't
unusual, Tebbutt said, for them to rise before dawn, put in a
full workday, and be at the bar by lunchtime, "drinking and
smoking pot all afternoon."

The next day they'd do it all over again.

Sometimes, Tim said, they'd start drinking while they
were at the track, a practice that was risky for a trainer or hotwalker, and downright suicidal if you were an exercise rider,
as well, which happened to be the case for Tim.

"I used to drink every day," he said. "Galloping horses in
the morning, I could drink five whiskeys, no problem, and then
close down the bar afterward. I mean every goddamn day,
the whole meet. But I quit all that when I met Lisa. Well, a little
earlier, actually, because I got a DWI six months before I met
Lisa, so I'd kind of made a decision on my own—or had it
forced on me, I guess you'd say."

He quit cold turkey. No rehab, no twelve-step meetings,
no meds to help with withdrawal symptoms. Just white-
knuckled it alone on the bathroom floor, sweating out all the
toxins, throwing up so hard he thought his ribs would break.

And then it was over.

A few weeks later he nearly ran down a pretty girl on the
shedrow, and for a while everything changed.

"I never really went back to that life," Tim said. "Lisa
wouldn't have stood for it. I got drunk on occasion, flicked
ashes into a shoe, thinking it was an ashtray, but that's not really a relapse. Not compared to the way I was. It's a bad habit,

don't get me wrong. But there's a big difference between going out and having a few drinks to celebrate when your horse wins, eating lobster tails like they're shrimp and washing them down with a good bottle of wine . . . that ain't the same thing as putting away a pint of whiskey while galloping horses. When Lisa came along I had started to clean up my act; and then all of a sudden I had someone to take care of. And she took care of me, too."

She'd always been a rescuer, drawn instinctively to people and animals that needed help; she couldn't stop herself. So while Tim might have been the older and more experienced person in their relationship, he was not necessarily the one in charge. They had a complicated union, one born of mutual need, each of them having been damaged in some way. If they were an unlikely couple and their courtship not exactly the stuff of fairy tales, it worked nonetheless.

"Their relationship was all about horses," said Cheryl Hall, Tim's sister. "That's how it began, and that's how it ended. But I know my brother, and he was madly in love with the sweetness and purity of Lisa. It's such an ugly world sometimes, and Timmy had seen his share of ugly things. He'd been through a lot, and he could be his own worst enemy. But then Lisa came along, and she was so wonderful; such a simple, beautiful girl. But a regular girl, you know? She'd had this head injury, and she'd had cancer . . . and none of it seemed to slow her down. She was the best thing that ever happened to Tim."

They quickly became inseparable, a development that amused and baffled Tim's friends.

"At one point Timmy put on a lot of weight," John Tebbutt

recalled. "He got so fat he could barely get out of his car. I'd go sit in the barn with Lisa—and I always gave her a big hug and kiss when I saw her—and I'd say, 'What the hell are you still doing with him? He's a pain in the ass.' Then I'd turn to Timmy and say, 'Why don't you go clean out the stalls or something? Stop making your girl do all the work!' He'd just laugh, tell me to fuck off, and then Lisa would laugh at the two of us.

"In some ways they had a dysfunctional relationship," Tebbutt went on. "Lisa was very motherly to Tim and let a lot roll off her shoulders; too much, probably. But she loved him dearly, and he adored her. She was a very kind, compassionate person. She saw through Timmy's bullshit, and she didn't really even care. Timmy's the kind of guy who probably shouldn't be married; he's too much of a handful. But we all look for love, don't we? We all look for someone to love us and take care of us. And that's as close as Timmy ever got or probably ever will get."

By the winter of 1994–95, Tim and Lisa had become partners in every sense of the word. Carol and Frank Calley had graciously welcomed Tim into their lives, primarily because he seemed to have a positive influence on their daughter's mood, and because they figured eventually the relationship would run its course. Hopefully, Lisa, having gotten some of the wildness out of her system, would settle back into a more normal life, preferably with someone closer to her own age and not quite so . . . *different*. Instead, the pair went off to Ocala to

gallop horses for John Candlin, a New York trainer and owner
who raced horses on the New York Racing Association circuit, as well as at Finger Lakes.

In March, as the winter season drew to a close, Tim and
Lisa decided to drive west to St. Petersburg for vacation. They
figured they'd spend a few weeks relaxing on the beach before heading home to Central New York, where winter would
not relent for another couple months. One morning, completely out of the blue, Lisa held Timmy's hand and asked him
a question:

"Can we get married?"

Although impulsive by nature, Tim was not prone to romantic gestures; nor had he ever demonstrated a propensity
for commitment. He was, in short, the kind of man you might
expect to hyperventilate at the very prospect of marriage. In
this case, though, the response came to him easily and without the slightest bit of doubt or dread:

"Hell, yeah, I'll marry you!"

He paused; then, in what can only be termed an act of
chivalry, he offered Lisa a chance to reconsider.

"Are you sure about this?"

She nodded. They embraced. A few hours later, on the
afternoon of March 13, 1995, Tim Snyder and Lisa Calley were
married at a courthouse in St. Petersburg, Florida. Two weeks
later they returned to New York and moved in with Lisa's parents. A month passed before they told anyone that they had
gotten married.

"And then Carol and Frank kicked us out of the house,"
Tim would say years later, laughing as he recounted the story.

"No, we didn't," Carol retorted. "We were happy for them."

She stopped, collected her thoughts, looked at Tim for a moment, and then continued. "He won me over because my daughter loved him and he was a horsey person. That was all it took."

Their venture became a family affair, with Carol eventually earning a groom's license and working alongside her daughter and son-in-law. If Tim could be irascible and impetuous, not unlike a horse or a small child, well, that wasn't such a terrible thing. No one was perfect, and whatever life Tim had led previously, he now seemed committed to Lisa, and to helping her find stability and happiness.

"She was a special girl, very warm and adventurous," Tim said. "She loved to travel, she loved the beach, and she loved to ride horses. What can I say? Lisa was my girlfriend, my wife, my partner—she covered all the bases. We were friends first, and then we fell for each other. I'd never felt like that about anyone before. She was a great person, very pure. The only thing she didn't have going for her was her health. I didn't know that much about her problems at first, but even when I found out, I didn't care. It didn't make a damn bit of difference to me."

Wanting a place of their own, but lacking the resources (or even the inclination) to buy a home, the couple moved together into a tack room at Finger Lakes. Essentially little more than a concrete bunker designed for transient and often penniless backstretch workers, it was the sort of accommodation that would make most newlyweds blanch; but it had exactly

the opposite effect on Tim and Lisa. Far from being saddened
or depressed by their humble surroundings, they were ener-
gized. What better way for a pair of horsemen to live? It cut
down on the commute, anyway. Get up in the morning, walk
out the door, go to work for the next sixteen hours, then grab
some sleep and do it all over again the next day.

Slowly, patiently, and with meager resources, they built a
business together over the next several years, working for
other trainers and owners while simultaneously acquiring and
selling inexpensive horses ("churning," as it's known in the
parlance of the business), sometimes racing their stock, sometimes not.

Their first project, foaled in January 1992 and purchased
by Tim and Lisa two years later, was a bay filly they dubbed
Lisa's Calley. She wasn't much of a horse, or didn't seem to be
anyway, on October 16, 1994, when she made her debut at
Finger Lakes in a maiden special weights race for juvenile fillies. The competition was light; nevertheless, Lisa's Calley
was completely overmatched. Starting in the third post position, in roughly the middle of a seven-horse field, with jockey
David Rivera aboard, she broke badly and wound up dead
last after only a few strides. By the time Rivera eased her
through the stretch, she was fifty-nine lengths behind, a rather
spectacular defeat in a race that spanned only five and a half
furlongs and was completed in slightly more than one min-
ute's time.

No matter. She was their horse—their only horse—and
they would not quit on her. She was named after Lisa, after all,
and hadn't the owner been an impressively resilient young

woman? Maybe the filly would, in time, display similar re-
solve. That's what made the game interesting—the possibility that a slow horse, given time and training and the right
guidance, might become suddenly fast. Breeding, the purists
would say, trumped everything in the end, but pragmatism
got you only so far when you toiled at the lower levels of the
sport. You had to have ambition and faith.

You had to have hope.

They took the filly to Florida when the racing scene shifted
south for the winter, gave her about ten weeks off to rest and
recuperate, and to grow into her body. In that sense, they
knew, horses were like people—some of them were perpet-
ual adolescents, taking months if not years to reach maturity
and perhaps blossom into functioning adults. Others, sadly,
never matured at all, and instead floundered in perpetuity.
This was the crux of the racing business: knowing when to
give up on a horse and when to stick with her. A rich owner
could indulge in sentiment; on the county fair circuit and at
second-tier tracks, where Tim and Lisa toiled, it was a luxury
few owners or trainers could afford. You had to be smart and
efficient; you had to be a shrewd businessman. Every so often,
though, you found a horse that made your heart beat faster,
and for those you were willing to bend the rules.

Lisa's Calley grew stronger with rest. She began working
in a pool, and after a few months returned to the track. Almost
immediately her handlers noticed that she appeared to be a different horse. More muscular, more confident. Lisa used to gallop the filly on a regular basis, until she became so rambunctious
and energetic that she couldn't be relied upon to do as she

was told. She wanted to run, and sometimes she wouldn't stop running. That was fine when you put her in the starting gate and asked her to race, but not such a good thing when the person riding her had a history of cancer and seizures. Lisa loved the horse, but eventually Tim convinced her to give up the saddle, except for leisurely strolls along the shedrow.

"I worried about her constantly," Tim said. "Lisa knew how to ride, and she loved galloping horses, but she wasn't always careful. There were certain things I did not allow her to do because they were just too dangerous for someone in her condition."

For example, one of the more challenging aspects of training a budding racehorse is acclimating the animal to a starting gate. Thoroughbreds are prickly, high-strung creatures by nature, and when you put them in an enclosed space and shut the door fore and aft, they tend to get agitated. Especially if they are new to the process.

It is a popular misconception that most racetrack injuries occur on the track, when horses collide or break down. Those are simply the most spectacular and catastrophic accidents, provoking as they often do injuries that can cripple or maim or even result in fatalities. Less shocking—in part because they occur mostly out of sight—but far more common are accidents that occur before the race even begins, as anxious animals are carefully steered into the starting gate.

Indeed, there are few moments in sports more intense than those that occur in the brief span between the final stall door closing and the bell that signals the start of a race. Ask just about any veteran jockey and they'll tell you this is the time when they worry the most about getting hurt, for all it takes is a slight buck for the rider to be pinned against the steel walls of the starting gate. If a horse loses his shit, so to speak, in that setting, it quickly becomes contagious, with one horse after another snorting and kicking and arching its back, trying to unseat his rider and fight his way to freedom. For this reason jockeys reserve a special disdain for the starter who is slow on the trigger, allowing horses to linger in the gate.

"Everyone who works around a racetrack knows the starting gate is the most dangerous place to work," said Tim Snyder. "You've got a thousand-pound horse, a hundred-pound jockey, and you're putting them both in a steel cage. Out on the track you can get thrown, but the ground is forgiving and even if you get trampled, you'll probably be okay. In the gate you can get absolutely crushed."

So Lisa stayed away from the starting gate, at least while Tim was in her orbit. Since they also worked for other trainers and owners, though, there were times when Lisa would be assigned tasks that Tim might not have permitted, and if he wasn't around to police the situation, well . . .

"She'd do it," Tim said. "She was that kind of girl. Not afraid of anything. But if I found out . . ."

On more than one occasion, Tim said, he lost jobs after confronting employers who had allowed Lisa to work their horses in the starting gate, or gallop a particularly boisterous animal. It didn't matter whether they knew of her condition, or even if she had volunteered for the assignment. Not to Tim. People took all sorts of silly risks at the racetrack—hell, he'd taken enough of them himself—but this was different. This was his wife, and no job, no paycheck, was worth her life.

•   •   •

The seizures came without warning and presented symptomatically in a variety of ways: a blank stare in response to a question might simply mean that Lisa wasn't listening closely or was otherwise distracted; then again, it might also mean that she was in the midst of a neurological episode of undetermined severity. In that sense, at least, the milder seizures were more difficult to comprehend than those that prompted physical contortions or loss of consciousness. Frank and Carol Calley had long ago learned to deal with the unpredictability of their daughter's medical condition, and while the more intense episodes still filled them with anguish, they no longer feared for her life.

Tim was another story.

It took time for him to adjust to Lisa's ongoing struggle, and to resist the urge to panic each time she suffered an episode. For a few years he was befuddled by the mysterious nature of her ailment, the way she could disappear into herself, falling into an almost peaceful trance. There was the afternoon, for instance, when Tim and Carol were sitting in the kitchen of the Calley home, talking casually at the end of a workday.

"All of a sudden you could hear something banging outside," Tim recalled. "Like footsteps. Big footsteps."

With a mother's intuition, Carol jumped to her feet and began walking to the back door. As she approached, she could see the head of a horse bobbing slowly up and down, in time with its stride. Carol opened the back door to find Lisa standing there, reins in hand, a distant look in her eye.

"She was trying to bring the horse into the house," Carol

recalled. "She had no idea what she was doing or where she was. But you know the funny thing? She had complete control over the horse. I guess she just decided it was time to come home, and she wanted to bring the horse with her."

Tim shook his head at the memory. "Craziest thing I ever saw. But I got used to it after a while."

The illness, Tim believes, brought them closer. They learned to fight through the episodes together, and to laugh at the challenges and misconceptions they sometimes provoked.

Early one morning Tim and Lisa were on their way to work at Beulah Park, a racetrack located in Grove City, Ohio, not far from Columbus. As Tim recalls the event, they were chatting and driving, enjoying their morning coffee as they approached the front gate, when Lisa suddenly fell silent.

"Her whole body tightened up," Tim said. "She clenched her fists and squeezed the coffee cup so hard it splashed all over the car, burned me in the face. I slammed the truck into neutral, tried to take her seat belt off while the engine was still running. But she was thrashing all over the place. I got her in a headlock with one arm, released the seat belt with the other. I was scared to death she was going to choke herself."

Over the course of the next few minutes, they rode out the seizure together, Lisa convulsing violently in Tim's arms. Eventually the shaking quelled and Tim loosened his grip, letting Lisa fall back against his chest. It was just about then that Tim heard a sound off in the distance, a sound he recognized as the feint whining of a siren. At first he paid it no mind, but then the screeching grew louder and as Tim looked up in the rearview mirror, with Lisa tucked into his embrace, he could see the flashing of lights and the unmistakable mono-tone markings of a police cruiser. He watched in disbelief as the officer approached the car, hand on holster, ready to do business.

If ever there was a situation that screamed to be misunderstood, Tim quickly realized, this was it.

"The son of a bitch working the security gate had called the cops," Tim explained. "He was used to seeing fights. Hell, everyone fights at the racetrack, and he just figured I was some guy beating the shit out of his girl. I guess you can't blame him. Lisa used to shake like crazy when she had a bad seizure, and I was on top of her. It probably looked pretty bad from a distance."

By the time the officer reached the truck, the convulsions had stopped, a crowd had gathered, and Lisa had regained consciousness. Together they explained what had happened. The officer asked if they needed medical assistance. No, Tim said. She just needed to sleep.

The officer nodded and walked away.

"It was embarrassing," Tim remembered. "Everyone felt bad. But that's just the way it was with Lisa. You never knew when she was going to have a seizure, and you never knew how bad they would be. We learned to deal with it the best we could."

If Tim frequently served as caregiver for Lisa, well, she certainly reciprocated. By all accounts she was every bit the workhorse that he was, and usually the more focused partner in their relationship. It was her nature to be calm, patient, organized, almost zenlike in her approach to life and work. And while Lisa's health problems were more pronounced,

Tim had his issues, as well, either as a result of hard living or simply because he spent so much time working with animals; periodically, the odds caught up with him.

Like the time at Finger Lakes, on a blustery day in the late 1990s, when Tim was riding one of his horses to the track for a workout.

"A Thursday," Tim recalled. "I remember that because Thursday was garbage day, and this one guy, another trainer, had dragged his empty feed bags outside the barn, and they weren't tied down or anything. Then the damn wind came up and got them bags in a swirl, and the horse reared up, knocked me off, fell on top of me, knocked the horse out cold. So I'm lying on the ground, pinned beneath him, and I'm in bad fuckin' shape. A whole bunch of people came running out, tried to lift the horse off me, but couldn't even budge him. They kicked him, they threw water on his face. Nothing."

For nearly twenty minutes they stood in a loose circle, waiting helplessly, impatiently for the animal to rouse itself and slide away.

"The last thing I remember was him getting up and continuing to step all over me," Tim said. "And in the process he punched holes in me everywhere. Just by walking away from me he did the most damage. Last thing I saw was the horse's tail and his head was turned, and he fell into a ditch across the street."

Tim had hit the ground so hard that his helmet had cracked in half. But it was his lower body that took the brunt of the accident.

"I couldn't walk," he said. "So Sammy Blake, a jockey's

agent, he got on one arm, and Lisa got on the other. I told Lisa to give me her flack jacket, since I wasn't wearing one and I didn't want to get in trouble when they started investigating. When the ambulance arrived, I told them I was fine, which wasn't true, of course. But I didn't have any health insurance— just workman's comp—so the last thing I needed was an ambulance bill and an emergency room visit."

They wound up at a nearby hotel, Tim soaking his battered legs in a bathtub filled with ice, tossing back Percodan with a six-pack of Genesee.

"Go back to the track, finish putting away the rest of the horses," Tim instructed his wife. "I'll be okay."

Within a few hours the painkillers and adrenaline had worn off and Lisa had returned to the hotel, finding her husband in a world of hurt. Gone was the facade of toughness, and with it any pretense of having avoided a serious injury or even concern about how they'd pay the crushing medical bills that would follow. Lisa helped Tim to his feet and virtually dragged him out to the parking lot and then drove him to a nearby hospital, where a shot of Demerol dulled the pain and X-rays revealed a pair of broken legs. Tim left the hospital several hours later in a wheelchair pushed by Lisa and casts up to his knees.

"This horse business—it's dangerous," Tim said. And it's not all glamorous. There's a lot of horseshit in the horse business. The public has no idea what we go through to get that picture in the winner's circle. If you're someone like Todd Pletcher or Bob Baffert, with two hundred head of stock and an army of folks working for you, maybe it's different. I don't know. I'm sure they work hard, too. But for most of us it's a really tough life. The thing that makes it worthwhile is having someone you can share it with. Someone to help you carry the load."

Chapter Six

In the beginning, John Shaw had been cautiously optimistic. A veteran horse broker with more than two decades of experience, he knew his business well, knew what to look for in a horse, and what to avoid. In a typical year he would acquire somewhere between fifty and seventy-five racehorses; virtually all of them would be sold to someone else. He was a racetrack middleman, a conduit between breeder and owner. If the formula was simple—buy low, sell high—the reality of his work was something else altogether. It was a complicated and risky venture, one dependent on weighing the strict calculus of bloodlines against the *horseman's hunch*—which was less about gambling than it was the hard-earned intuition gleaned through an endless series of predawn workouts and the occasional heart-stopping surprise.

Like most horse brokers, Shaw knew better than to be

ruled by his heart. He was, in many ways, no different than a Wall Street trader, with horseflesh his chosen investment vehicle. Stock was acquired and moved with ruthless precision. At all levels of racing, brokers are a quiet but active part of the thoroughbred industry, finding owners for horses that aspire to greatness and for those that will settle for much less.

"Every racehorse is a lottery ticket," Shaw said. "In the end, when I move a horse, I just want to make sure it has a home. I want to know that it's not going to be put down just because it can't run."

That happens sometimes, unfortunately. A racehorse that can't race, or can't race well enough, is an economic sinkhole. It is a common misperception that the sport of thoroughbred horse racing is populated only by men and women with extraordinarily deep pockets, casually and even recklessly tossing money at an expensive hobby. Far more common, especially when you dig below the elite levels of the sport, are owners who consider five figures a prohibitive amount to invest in an animal as fickle as a racehorse. Transactions in which only a few thousand dollars change hands are actually quite common; sometimes, horses are literally given away.

Such was the case with the big bay filly that had been foaled and raised at Ocala Stud, before finding its way to John Shaw.

"She was a good-looking horse, big and strong, with a decent pedigree. Not great, but respectable," Shaw remembered. "But when I tried to work her? Jesus Christmas, she was slow. I practically had to time this horse with a sundial. It was ridiculous."

Unsure what to do, and encouraged even on the worst

days by the sheer attractiveness of the animal—*God, there must be a racehorse in there somewhere!*—Shaw hung unto the horse for more than six months. There was no way to break the mystery, to figure out what was in the filly's head that made her so reluctant to run. To Shaw, she appeared structurally sound. Yes, there was a small, irregular patch of white on her left eye, like snowflakes against a night sky, and that sort of thing when seen in a racehorse can indicate impaired vision (and indeed future owners of the filly would claim that she was nearly blind in that eye). But when Shaw approached the filly from the left side, she would respond appropriately; when he waved a hand across the left side of her head, she would flinch. Good signs, to be sure.

"She looked fabulous when I got her, and she looked fabulous when she left here," Shaw said. "She came from Ocala Stud, which is the premiere farm in Florida; and Florida is the largest horse manufacturer on the planet. Ocala Stud is a tremendous farm. This filly had every opportunity. She had all her shots, she was wormed, fed properly, pampered from Day One. Her whole life was perfect."

For whatever reason, though, when Shaw would lead her out to the track for a morning workout, he was subjected to the same sort of discouraging performance that had led Michael O'Farrell to unload the horse in the first place. It wasn't that she was injured; it wasn't that she was overweight or undernourished; it wasn't that she lacked the physical tools to run, and to run well. The way Shaw saw it, she was simply lazy. Her effort was almost comically lackluster.

"This filly would get beat by twenty-five lengths going three-eighths of a mile," Shaw recalled. "She couldn't beat any horse on the farm. Why? Who knows? I think with some horses it's in their breeding. They don't train at all, or they don't train well, and they go to the track and they drop out of the gate, and it's a whole new ball game. Suddenly they run. Or it can work the other way. That's the funny thing about horses. You can buy a racing prospect and it works fast all the time, and you get all excited. You think, Wow, this horse can really run. No, not necessarily. It can *train*. Until you put it in a race, you never know. You can pay three hundred thousand dollars for a horse that's training like a champ, enter it in a race, and it can't beat anybody. And I'm talking about running for seventy-five hundred bucks against maidens at Penn National.

"Just because a horse can run, or train, does not mean that it can race. It might have the ability to run just as fast as everyone else—or faster—but it can't race, or won't race. There are plenty of horses working at Penn National or Finger Lakes, every day, putting in workouts that are just as fast as the horses at Belmont. But they can't race; that's why they're at Finger Lakes. And every once in a while you see just the opposite—a horse that hates to train, but when you put it in the gate, her genetic wherewithal kicks in, and the pedigree comes out, and she becomes a racehorse. She has the ability and the competitive desire. It's just that in the morning, for some reason, without the crowd and the environment and the starting gate and all the shit that goes with it, she's a nag. That's the only way I can explain what happened with this horse. Because in the morning she was unbelievably slow. Honestly? I didn't think she had any ability whatsoever."

Like Michael O'Farrell, Shaw was so thoroughly unimpressed by the bay filly that he felt conflicted about even trying to sell her. Any exchange of currency, he reasoned, was going to leave the buyer feeling as though he'd been cheated.

"I figured whoever got her would end up getting mad at me," Shaw said. "She was that slow."

As a compromise, Shaw put in a call to an acquaintance named Don Hunt, who also trained and brokered horses for a living.

"My deal with Don was, 'Come and get her, try to do something with her. I gotta tell you, though, she's so slow you have to mark the ground to make sure she's moving. But maybe you've got some people—you have more clients than I do, that's for sure—so maybe you know someone who would want her.' I had no expectations. If Don had told me he found some little girl who wanted to take her and use her as a jumping horse, that would have been fine with me. This horse was so slow that even if someone fell off her they wouldn't get hurt."

In November 2009, Don Hunt drove with a friend to Shaw's training center in Ocala to take a look at the World's Slowest Filly. Like Shaw and O'Farrell, they were impressed by the horse's size and stature, but concerned about her dismal training record, as well as the spot on her eye and what Hunt thought was a structural imbalance in her feet. But there was enough upside in the horse's pedigree and physical appearance that Hunt was willing to take a chance on her. He'd work with the filly, make any adjustments that were necessary in terms of shodding, and in a couple months try to find a buyer. If all went well, he and Shaw would split the profit.

If there *was* any profit, which was far from a guarantee.

"Her feet were atrocious, and I swear she was blind in that one eye," Hunt recalled. "But she still looked great. And we worked on her. I had X-rays taken and we shod her three times over the next couple months. But I never thought she'd turn out to be much of a horse. Hell, I never even put a saddle on her."

A few weeks after Hunt acquired the horse from Shaw, the two men chatted on the phone.

"Donny, is she getting any better?" Shaw asked.

Hunt laughed, as if it were the most ridiculous question.

"No, she's not."

"Okay," Shaw said, more than a trace of resignation in his voice. "Do whatever you want with her."

Chapter Seven

Remember the horse we claimed at Brockton? He stood out like something I was supposed to have. He has had a greater purpose than to be just a racehorse; he was like a gift from God, given at a time when I needed something to hope for, to live for. I have made this incredible journey on the wings of friends and family who have prayed and have had their prayers answered. I believe that being sick has been an opportunity for God to reveal Himself, not only to me, but to everyone I know! This has been a time of awakening for all of us . . . There are still a few bumps in the road, and the doctor keeps coming up with some new ailment whenever I see him—I'm contemplating finding a new doctor who will tell me what I want to hear:

"Go back to work!"

—Lisa Calley, March 2003

They built their business slowly, overcoming meager funds with hard work and an almost playful approach to the racing game. Well, Lisa was playful, anyway. Tim was mostly irascible and narrow-minded—a "my way or the highway" kind of guy—which is why they complemented each other nicely. They never made a lot of money, but in time they nurtured and developed a healthy little enterprise that typically was home to between one and two dozen horses, some of which they raced, some of which they simply bought and sold. In their time together, Tim estimates, he and Lisa churned nearly five hundred horses.

Their base of operations—their *home*—was in Central New York, but they traveled frequently and with little baggage. They'd spend part of the summer in Canada, racing at Fort Erie Racetrack in Ontario; in the winter they'd move to Florida. And there were stops all along the way, at tracks large and small (but mostly small)—anywhere they could pick up a claimer or find a buyer for one of theirs.

"They had cheap horses, but they had quite a few of them," said John Tebbutt. "You know—thousand-dollar horses. Maybe two thousand. They'd deal all over the place: Finger Lakes, Beulah, the county fair circuit; anyplace they could find a healthy, inexpensive horse. I hate to use the term 'bottom feeders,' but that's the one that keeps popping into mind. And the truth is, there's a lot of people in this industry who operate that way. You do the best you can with the resources you have. And they treated their stock well. To Timmy it was a business. Horses were a product, a means to survive. That's the way he was raised, and that's the way he supported himself for a number of years; he couldn't afford to get attached to a horse. But Lisa was different. She absolutely loved her horses."

It's an unusual relationship horsemen have with their stock, one rooted in the practicalities of business and finance, but complicated by emotion. There is, for example, no sadder sight at a racetrack than that of a jockey frantically easing his mount through the stretch, pulling at the reins, working with all his might to stop an animal that has already broken down. While some incidents that result in equine fatality are spectacular—crowded stretch runs in which exhausted, fiercely competitive animals clip heels and tumble to the dirt, dragging helpless riders in their wake—many are deceptively quiet. A seemingly healthy colt, in the throes of mid-race oxygen debt and lactic acid accumulation, begins to weaken beneath the strain.

Sometimes the jockey can feel this happening; he uses instinct and experience to gauge the amount of fuel left in the tank, and whether the whip is necessary or even practical. It is his job to push the horse, to exact every ounce of speed and ability and competitiveness in an effort to win the race. But he also bears the burden of responsibility, of knowing when to pull back so that the horse suffers no long-term damage. Usually it's just a matter of understanding that there really is no point in beating a dead (or exhausted) horse. Sometimes, though, more nefarious forces are at work: an undiagnosed stress fracture, perhaps, or a strained tendon; anything that might cause the animal to take a bad step and go down. The thoroughbred racehorse is a miraculous animal, an architectural marvel that almost looks like an evolutionary mistake: so much bone and muscle and mass supported by the spindliest of foundations. That it works as well as it does, as often as it does, is something of a mystery.

Every so often, though, the engineering reveals its flaws, and a catastrophic breakdown is the result. Some we remember—the magnificent filly Ruffian suffering a compound fracture of her right ankle in a match race with Kentucky Derby winner Foolish Pleasure at Belmont Park in the summer of 1975—most we don't. Regardless of the venue, the purse, the size of the audience, what follows a racetrack breakdown is a well-orchestrated death march familiar to anyone who has spent much time around the sport. An equine ambulance appears on the track, a screen is erected around the fallen animal, and a lethal injection is quietly administered. Then the carcass is hauled away and the show goes on.

It is this aspect of the business that riles animal rights groups, provokes feelings of guilt in spectators, and weakens the knees of owners, jockeys, and trainers. But if you are around the game long enough, you understand death is a cost of doing business. Some people—trainers, mostly—steel themselves against the sadness by refusing to allow themselves to get close to their stock. Ask a veteran trainer how he feels when a horse is put down, and he might tell you that it hurts; he might also tell you that it's no big deal.

"It's just a damn horse."

"That's true," Tebbutt said. "Some people are like that. Not me. I have a different attitude about it. When I have to put a horse down, I hold it in my arms. I'm in love with the horse, not the game. Lisa was like that, too. Timmy wasn't. He was very good with horses, an excellent horseman who understood and appreciated his animals. But he did not allow himself to get attached to them. Lisa couldn't help herself. She was so kind and compassionate to everyone—including her horses. She loved them all, whether they could make money or not."

If theirs was a life unrecognized and unwanted by the blue bloods of the thoroughbred racing world, it was a happy and successful life nonetheless. Lisa and Tim were professional horsemen; they were owners and trainers. For them, that was enough.

"The horses became her children," observed Carol Calley. "We didn't talk about it too much, but I know she always wanted to have kids; she just couldn't because of all her health problems. That always made me sad, because Lisa would have been a wonderful mother."

Added Tim: "We talked about adopting. Then, with a laugh, he added, "Well, Lisa talked about it, mainly. She told me one day, 'We're gonna find us an orphanage, go adopt a couple kids about fifteen years old, and get them to do all the work!' She was kidding, of course. I think she missed having children and that's why she threw all her energy into the horses. I mean, I like horses, but Lisa *loved* them. And she took care of them like they were children."

Like children, horses require a combination of love, discipline, and patience to reach a healthy level of maturity. Unlike children, they need custodial care throughout their lives, a fact ignored by most racing fans, who are either too enamored of the beauty of the sport or too busy chasing a gambling buck to recognize the grit beneath the surface.

"Horses require constant care," Tim noted with a solemnity born of experience. "You ever look at a horse's feet?

Probably not. Who the hell looks at a horse's feet, unless you own one. Well, let me tell you, they're packed with shit. Not just dirt and mud, but shit. Horseshit. They crap all over the place and stomp around in it, and every day you have to get in there and pick it out; if you don't, they're gonna get sick. You want a horse with thrush? Don't clean the shit out of its shoes. Then the whole barn gets sick, and pretty soon you're out of business. Lisa understood that part of it, too. It doesn't matter how pretty they are, they're still horses, and what goes on at the barn in the morning is what really matters. All that other stuff—the braided tail, the colorful silks, the guy wearing a suit in the paddock, in the afternoon, before the race? That's all window dressing."

They waited damn near too long to reconnect.

Warren Snyder had moved to the West Coast in the late 1970s. At the time he was broke and broken, drinking himself into an alcoholic stupor on most days and seemingly bent on following his wife to an early exit. If not for an extraordinary effort on the part of his daughter, he might well have succeeded. Through an intermediary in Boston, she found her father, managed to get him on a plane bound for San Diego, and picked him up at the airport, still reeling from his latest bender. Cheryl took him in with no real plan, not knowing then that he would spend the last twenty years of his life under her roof. But she adapted to his presence and his needs, converting a garage into an apartment and creating a home for the father she barely knew. Slowly he came around, his health and temperament improving with the passing of time.

Tim kept his distance from all of this, had no real interest in seeing the old man or forgiving him or engaging in any
cathartic reconciliation. They were at opposite ends of the
country, separated by three thousand miles and a lifetime of
anger. Tim had a decent life now. He had a business. He had a
barn full of horses. He had a wife and friends and family. And
if sometimes he wasn't the easiest guy in the world to get along
with, well, at least he was loyal. He didn't run at the slightest
inconvenience or flare. Not anymore. It had taken most of his
adult life, but that influence, at least—the urge to flee—he had
learned to shake.

The old man had dried out? Good for him. Tim was happy
for his father and proud of his sister. She was strong and compassionate. She had patience, frankly, that Tim couldn't imagine. But he didn't need to be part of his father's resurrection.
He had his own life and his own responsibilities. There was
no need to complicate matters.

One day, though, in 1998, Cheryl called to tell Tim that
their father was sick. He had colon cancer; had it for some
time, in fact. If Tim had any interest in seeing the old man before he died, now would be a good time to make some plans.
So Tim gave it some thought and decided to acquiesce. His
mother had died in estrangement; no point in letting things
end the same way with his father. Lisa wanted to make the
trip with him. She'd heard a batch of wild stories over the
years, but had never met Warren Snyder. She wanted to know
a little bit more about her husband's past, about the family
tree from which he'd fallen.

Not a chance, Tim told her. You don't need to be part
of this.

"He was dying of cancer and so skinny and sick. Lisa had enough of her own problems, with the seizures and cancer. I didn't want her to see him like that. I knew it would be too scary for her."

But there was something else that drove Tim's decision, something a bit less noble than a desire to shield or protect his wife. For the very same reason that Lisa wanted to meet Warren Snyder—curiosity over her husband's background— Tim wanted to prevent that meeting. She loved him and respected him and cared for him; maybe, he thought, if she meets my father, something will change. Then she'll know what I'm really like, and what I'm destined to become, both physically and emotionally.

"My dad had been on borrowed time for a few years by the time I saw him," Tim recalled. "He wasn't a drunk anymore, and at least he'd learned how to function. But he was still my father. On one hand I was proud of him for the rider he was and what he'd accomplished. But on the other hand . . ."

Tim's voice trailed off. He searched for the right words.

"I guess I was embarrassed to say, 'That's my father.'"

Yet, as it turned out, the things that shamed and frightened Tim—Warren's diminished state and checkered past— were overshadowed by what he perceived as strength in those waning days.

"Christ, he weighed fifty-one pounds when he died," Tim said. "Just disgusting, a sack of bones. But he wouldn't give up. By the time I got there he was beyond any sort of treatment. He'd been through chemo and all that, and they were just trying to keep him comfortable, had him hooked up to IV bags filled with fluids and painkillers 'round the clock."

For several days Tim sat by his father's side, sharing old stories, showing him videotaped footage of races featuring horses that he and Lisa had bought over the years. Warren was under hospice care at the time, and one day a nurse approached Tim with a smile of admiration.

"Your father is the toughest man I've ever met," she said. Tim nodded.

You're goddamn right he is.

She was sick before anyone realized it.

That's one of the challenges faced by someone who suffers from a seizure disorder: "sick" is normal and not necessarily even cause for alarm. It's a challenge for their families, as well. They grow accustomed to the disruptions, to events that might seem frightening and traumatic to the uninitiated. Lisa was by nature a strong and optimistic person, prone to offering reassurance to those around her even as she endured pain and discomfort and unpredictability. She was not inclined to share her concern when a new symptom presented itself, or a seizure strayed from the usual course. Those closest to her were forever trying to squelch the urge to ask if she was okay, and to intrude on her independence, for always the response was the same:

I'm fine . . . don't worry.

In 2001 Lisa and Tim rented a town house within walking distance of Beulah Park. It would be their base of operations for the duration of the meet, and they treated it with the appropriate degree of indifference.

"We were hardly ever there," Tim remembered. "We

were always at the track, so we basically left it empty. There was a double-wide couch in the living room, covered with white leather—looked like something you'd find in a doctor's office—and we pushed it into the bedroom and slept on it. It was fine. We didn't need much."

The couple hadn't been there more than two weeks when Lisa suffered some sort of neurological episode. Tim was downstairs at the time; Lisa was in an upstairs bathroom, getting ready for bed. Tim could hear a faucet in use, and at first thought nothing of it. But then the water continued to run.

Five minutes.

Ten minutes.

Ever frugal, and easily irritated by the thought of money running down the drain, Tim went upstairs to investigate. He walked into the bathroom and found the sink half-filled with water, the faucet wide open, toothpaste splattered everywhere: across the porcelain, the floor, and the walls. Tim turned off the water and began anxiously tracing the toothpaste trail down the hall.

"Lisa?" he said.

There was no response.

Streaks and puddles of toothpaste led him first to the bedroom, and then finally into a closet, where he found Lisa slumped to the floor, a wet toothbrush by her side.

"Damndest thing," Tim said. "Must have had a seizure while she was brushing her teeth, then turned and walked all the way into the bedroom, and then fallen into the closet. Who knows? She didn't remember anything."

It struck Tim as he picked up the toothbrush how lucky she had been, how random these things were, and how circumstances wildly beyond anyone's control could determine not only the severity of a seizure, but the consequences that would follow. What if she had swallowed the toothbrush? What force had intervened to prevent her from choking to death . . . or hitting her head instead of slumping benignly to the floor?

Fate?

Luck?

Tim could only shake his head and hold his wife and wait for her to come around, as she always did. Then everything would be fine.

The following morning Lisa went back to work, joining her husband at the barn despite his protestations. She dutifully went through the day's chores, but Tim noticed she was less animated than usual. He asked if she was okay. She nodded, explained that she was a little tired but otherwise fine.

The next day he noticed a hitch in her step. Occasionally she would roll her shoulders as if trying to release tension; sometimes she'd rub the small of her back. With growing unease, Tim watched her struggle to get through the day. Before they left the track, he made a decision.

"Pack your shit," he told his wife. "We're going home."

At first they thought that Lisa's problems were limited to malfunctioning kidneys—a result, perhaps, of her previous battle with cancer or her ongoing struggle with seizure disorder. She'd spent a lifetime, it seemed, under the care of physicians, her body absorbing near-toxic levels of medication, all filtered through the kidneys and liver. It wasn't uncommon for patients in Lisa's condition to experience systemic break-down of one sort of another, and that seemed to be the most likely scenario. It wasn't a good thing, of course, but it beat the alternative: a return of the cancer that had nearly killed her a decade earlier.

In April 2002, after many months of feeling lethargic and vaguely ill, Lisa underwent a procedure in which a stent was inserted into her lower back in an effort to rescue her failing kidneys. But she continued to wither, prompting a second round of surgery at the end of May, this one far more aggressive and, ultimately, revealing.

"They called it exploratory surgery," Carol remembered. She paused, letting the full weight of that word—*exploratory*—sink in. "It was supposed to last forty-five minutes, but it ended up being six hours. It was a full hysterectomy . . . and a lot more."

Afterward—after she had nearly died on the table—doctors explained that the cancer had returned and metastasized. There were tumors throughout her back and abdomen, pressing against her kidneys and liver, invading space that was intended to be occupied by healthy organs. The surgeons had carefully excised as much of the marauding tissue as possible, but further treatment would be necessary if Lisa was to beat back the disease again. So they sent her home to recover, to regain her strength before embarking on the second phase of the battle: radiation and chemotherapy. She endured both in the sweltering summer months of 2002; a series of scans afterward revealed that all of the tumors had been destroyed. For the time being, Lisa was cancer-free.

It didn't last. By Thanksgiving the cancer had taken root again. Another round of chemotherapy and radiation was recommended, this one much more potent.

"It was awful," Tim said. "First they practically cut the poor kid in half, then they nearly kill her with chemo. She'd be sick for five hours after the treatments, throwing up so hard she almost passed out."

A habitual list-maker and note-taker, Lisa kept a journal of sorts during those months, just as she had for much of her life. What's interesting is not what the journal reveals, but what it does not reveal. Rather than a grisly, depressing, blow-by-blow account of a young woman's combat against cancer, it is for the most part a collection of thoughts and notations on the daily minutiae of life, as experienced by a horse trainer, scribbled on the pages of a three-by-five-inch flip calendar:

> *January 3—Snowed all last night into today. Roads were bad.*
> *January 6—Mom and I went to Grandma's for dinner.*
> *January 7—Cielo rode beautifully. He's really beginning to figure out how to carry himself balanced!*

Then, on January 9, there are descriptions of horses brought out of the barn, a typical morning's work, followed by this:

> *Came home and got sick. Throwing up all afternoon. I stayed in bed and felt better by 9!*

There it is—the exclamation point (literal and meta-phorical) at the end of a brutal day. Not a "fuck you" to cancer—that wasn't her nature—but more of a thank-you offered for another day survived, another little fight won.

By February Lisa had completed her treatment and been given a reasonably clean bill of health. She felt good enough to make a trip to Florida with Tim, who had thrown himself into work as a means of coping, both financially and emotionally, with his wife's illness. As he had in years past, Tim began selling off horses and filling his days behind the wheel of a horse van, a hired hand hauling stock all over the Eastern Seaboard. It allowed him to feel useful, put some much-needed cash into their dwindling bank account, and (when he was honest with himself) it gave him an excuse to avoid some of the grim reality of living with a cancer patient.

"It was hard for Timmy to see her so sick," Carol said. "He's not good with that kind of stuff."

By the springtime, Lisa's blond hair had grown back and she'd regained enough of her strength to put in full days at the barn on her parents' property, where she and Tim now lived. A scan on March 26 showed no new tumors; there was, however, a small spot on her lung. Probably nothing, the doctors said, but they'd have to keep an eye on things. A follow-up scan on April 15 revealed another spot, this one in her pelvic region. The doctors gave her a choice: continue to monitor the situation, or undergo another round of chemo.

She chose to wait.

May 3—Funny Cide, New York–bred gelding, won the Kentucky Derby today!

May 8—Tim left this morning to pick up three horses at Pimlico and bring them to N.Y.C. One of the horses is an asshole. He fought on the trailer!
May 16—Tim arrived home around noon. He brought Mom a cute little mini-goat; she has long horns and likes to butt!

Journal entries throughout late May and early June focus heavily on friends and family, as well as Lisa's devotion to her favorite horse, Cielo's Surprise. There are numerous entries about her husband, and her concern over his health. Tim had grown almost obese during this period, a result of twenty-hour days as a long-haul trucker fueled by mountains of coffee, soda, and junk food. And all that time spent in such close proximity to horses had also resulted in Tim picking up some sort of nasty parasite—lice or fleas, most likely. They ravaged his skin, destroyed his clothes, and left him unable to sleep, a dangerous condition for a man driving 800 miles at a stretch.

In print, at least, Lisa fretted endlessly about Tim's health and safety, while wasting little time on her own deteriorating condition. By early summer, though, she knew something was seriously wrong. With increasing frequency she suffered bouts of heartburn and gastroenteritis. While out in the barn, working her horses, she noticed a nagging soreness in her back and shoulder. There were more hospital visits and scans, one of which showed a significant tumor blossoming in her abdomen.

July 25—I went to University Hospital for a check-up. They said I could get the tumor in my stomach radiated. I said I'd rather wait till winter. I told them to make sure

*and see "Seabiscuit" the movie! Tracy (the M.D.) said she
is going this weekend!*

Over the course of the next month Lisa continued to
weaken. There were more scans and tests, this time offering
irrefutable evidence that the cancer was spreading, and that
she had little choice but to engage the fight once again.

*August 20—It has been recommended for me to do the
chemotherapy. The tumor in the left side of my abdomen
is bigger, and there is a tumor near my rectum. The tumor
in my lung is starting to affect my breathing. In general—
I'm falling apart.*

That entry was precipitated by a visit to an oncologist, during
which Lisa was told that if she did not begin treatment, she
likely would have only a few months to live. Even with treatment, the prognosis was not encouraging. She was accompanied to the office by her mother (Tim was on the road once
again). Sitting in the doctor's office, the two of them took in
the words and held each other tightly, and began to cry.

"She had fought so hard, and been through so much, but
that was devastating news," Carol Calley remembered. "She
didn't want to give up, but the treatment was so harsh, and it
had taken so much out of her the last time. She couldn't imagine going through it all over again."

Two days later Lisa received a phone call from Tim's sister, Cheryl, who, after thirty years in California had become
something of a devotee of wellness and alternative therapies.

She invited Lisa to come out for a visit, get to know some of her in-laws, and try some holistic healing while she was there.

"I believe I will," Lisa wrote in her journal.

"I don't have any formal training, but I have a belief," Cheryl said years later, reflecting on that invitation. "I think doctors are great for surgery and for many other things. But sometimes, after you reach a certain point, they become drug pushers. There are other ways to do things."

Lisa's journal entries for August 23 through August 26 are lengthy and descriptive, filled with the excitement of a woman who is either still hopeful or tidying up loose ends. She rushes about, completing chores, working her horses, going shopping, sharing dinner with friends and family.

On August 26, 2003, she penned her final entry:

I leave for San Diego at 4:40 p.m. Have to be at airport one hour early.

Two weeks—that was the plan. Then she'd be home. But Lisa found that she enjoyed the company of her sister-in-law and her new, extended family, many of whom she had never met before, or had met only briefly. She liked the sunshine and the ocean breeze, and she embraced the alternative treatments that were offered to her: the wheat grass smoothies, colonics, and vitamin C drips. If she was desperate or depressed, well, she did a good job of hiding it, Cheryl thought. Lisa was enthusiastic about her treatment, and on the good days she seemed optimistic about the future.

"The best thing about Lisa coming out here was that we all got to know her," Cheryl said. "She had come out once before, for my daughter's wedding, but that was short. This time we really got to be together, and it was wonderful. I mean, it was sad, too, of course. She had been through so much, and she didn't want any more treatments. Had she been a bigger believer in what I was trying to do for her, and started earlier, she might have fared a little better; it's hard to say. She came so late in the game—cancer, stage 4. Her stomach was distended, and she couldn't eat a lot, and I'm making her juice drinks and whatever, but she just wanted to eat pizza. I think she was at a point where she just wanted to get away from all this stuff that had happened to her. So we would sit at the table and talk for hours on end, sometimes about her illness, but about a lot of other stuff, too. Lisa was a private person, and her parents are very private and quiet. They're wonderful people. But cancer is a horrible, lonely, isolating disease, and sometimes you need to talk to someone about it. Maybe I was that person for Lisa. I don't know. But I do know that I'm grateful for the time we had together."

That time was more extensive than anyone had anticipated. Days turned into weeks, weeks into months. If Lisa wasn't exactly thriving in her new environment, well, she wasn't getting any worse, either. If she was happy in California, everyone figured, then let her stay there as long as she liked.

In November, though, Lisa suffered a seizure that resulted in hospitalization. Doctors at Scripps Hospital in Encinitas, concerned over her seriously compromised condition, encouraged Lisa to be admitted for observation even after the seizure had passed. Carol and Tim flew out to California, unsure of what to do, or even what they might find when they arrived.

"It was strange," Tim remembered. "I thought she looked like the picture of health—smiling, happy."

"We knew she was very sick," Carol said, "but when we first got there, she didn't seem that bad. She was walking the halls of the hospital, eating, talking. A week later she was bedridden, couldn't walk at all. She went downhill very quickly, and we knew we had to make arrangements to bring her home, but we weren't sure how we were going to do that."

Tim was going to fly back first, thinking he would pick up their truck and drive straight back across the country. Then he would reverse course, with Lisa sleeping in the backseat. But that seemed neither prudent nor safe. In the end they enlisted the services of an agency that specialized in the transportation of seriously ill patients. Tim and Carol traveled on one flight, while Lisa traveled first class on another flight, accompanied by a private nurse.

"We were so fortunate to find them," Carol said. "I don't know what we would have done otherwise. The trip was hard, and Lisa had a bad accident on the way back, but the nurse took care of everything. We were waiting for them at the airport when they arrived, and I remember the look on Lisa's face as the nurse was pushing her in the wheelchair. She was smiling and waving, like she didn't want anyone to worry about her."

At home in Camillus, New York, in the same house where she had spent much of her life, Lisa moved into a first-floor bedroom so that her parents and husband, with help from hospice, could care for her more easily. There was no more discussion of "treatment" or "therapy," only quiet resolution and a determination to fill the days with as much normalcy as possible. Unable to walk, she'd sometimes ask to be wheeled outside, even in bad weather, so that she could be near her horses.

By Thanksgiving Lisa was virtually bedridden, but she still wanted friends and family to come to the Calley home for a holiday meal. That day, while Carol was busily preparing dinner, the strangest thing happened.

"A chicken hawk flew through the living room window," she recalled. "Smashed right through the glass and landed on the floor in front of the TV. I don't know how it happened, whether it was chasing a squirrel or something and lost its bearings, but it wound up right on our floor."

You see a hawk in flight and it's an impressive thing, the way it swoops and glides, floating effortless on the current. But to see one out of context, spread out in your home, is something else entirely. The Calley family watched the hawk twitch for a moment, its great wings fluttering feebly against expiration, marveling at its size and strength, and at the utter weirdness of the whole thing.

"I got Lisa out of bed so she could see it," Tim said. "We couldn't believe it. We were all speechless."

It occurred to Carol as they disposed of the carcass and cleaned up the glass that there might be something more to the hawk's demise than a mere aeronautical miscalculation. She had spent her whole life in Central New York, a region thick with Native American influence and folklore, and she couldn't shake the nagging sensation that greater forces were at work. What was it she had read? Something about a hawk's symbolic significance, that it was considered a spiritual messenger of some sort. And weren't birds, in all types of mythology, sometimes seen as escorts for souls moving from one world to the next?

"Probably just a coincidence," Carol said. "But it was very strange."

The last month was the worst, as Lisa's body deteriorated to a state of utter dependency. Heavy and frequent doses of morphine dulled the pain, but left her exhausted and confused. She stopped eating, declined a feeding tube, and withered to less than ninety pounds. Tumors in her spine impinged upon nerves and left her unable to walk or control her bodily functions.

"It was such a strain to see my daughter like that," Carol said. "Moaning at night, hurting so badly, unable to do anything for her. Thank God for the hospice people. I don't know what we would have done without them."

Tim had spent much of the previous year running from the harsh reality of his wife's condition, thinking perhaps that if he just kept moving, kept working, something would change. But now he slowed down. When people visited the house to speak with Lisa he would hide out in his room or go for a long, solitary drive. His grief and fear were his alone, and he felt no obligation to share them with anyone else. When the house was quiet, though, he would sit and talk with Lisa for hours on end, holding her hand, sharing stories of the horses they had bought and raised and sold. Once a day he would pick her up and carry her to the bathroom and gently slide her into the tub. Then he would wash her and dress her, and bring her back to her bed.

"I used to worry so much about them," Carol said. "Timmy was big and fat at the time, and he had a bad ankle, too. I thought he might drop her. But he needed to take care of her. And I know she wanted him to do it."

John Tebbutt saw a different side of Tim during that period; he saw a strength in his friend that he wasn't sure existed.

"When Lisa was dying, he did everything he could do," Tebbutt observed. "Tim did every single thing possible for her. He stayed with her the whole time. Anything she needed, wherever she needed to go, he was always right there for her. No matter what the situation was. Maybe that's the way it's supposed to be, but the truth is, not everyone is capable of it. It takes strength. It's admirable."

One night in the middle of December, while Carol sat beside her daughter's bed, exhausted and filled with sadness, Lisa looked at her mother and smiled.

"It's okay, Mom," she said. "I'm still going to be here."

Carol reached out and stroked her daughter's forehead.

"Really," Lisa added. "I'm coming back as a horse, and I'm going to lie down before you."

Carol didn't say much of anything in response, didn't give it much of a thought at the time.

"I don't know what that meant, really," Carol said after recounting the story. "I mean, she was on a lot of medication, so I didn't put too much stock into anything she was saying at the time. I think she was trying to comfort me. We were very close. We always went to the barn together, had a lot of fun together. Lisa wasn't just my daughter—she was my best friend, and I think I was her best friend."

Teenage jockey Warren Snyder in the winner's circle at Rockingham Park, after riding Septime to victory in November 1940. *(Photo courtesy Tim Snyder)*

Septime crosses the finish line first at Rockingham, with Warren Snyder aboard. *(Photo courtesy Tim Snyder)*

Warren Snyder weighs in before a race. *(Photo courtesy Tim Snyder)*

Warren Snyder and his wife, Virginia Snyder, relaxing on the beach with their infant son, Tim. *(Photo courtesy Tim Snyder)*

Timmy Snyder with his dad. *(Photo courtesy Tim Snyder)*

Timmy Snyder and his older sister, Cheryl, playing in the backyard of the Snyder home. *(Photo courtesy Tim Snyder)*

Tim Snyder, in his late teens, on yet another road trip. *(Photo courtesy Tim Snyder)*

Fearless from the start, little Lisa Calley begins a lifelong love affair with horses. *(Photo courtesy Tim Snyder)*

A teenage Lisa Calley competes in a jump competition. *(Photo courtesy Tim Snyder)*

Carol Calley and her daughter, Lisa, on vacation near Lake George, New York, in the 1980s. *(Photo courtesy Tim Snyder)*

Lisa Calley works with a horse at the family's indoor training facility in Camillus, New York. *(Photo courtesy Tim Snyder)*

Lisa and Tim relax during a trip to California. *(Photo courtesy Tim Snyder)*

Tim and Lisa at the wedding reception of Tim's niece, in California. *(Photo courtesy Tim Snyder)*

Lisa's Booby Trap crosses the finish line first to win the Loudonville Stakes at Saratoga Race Course on August 6, 2010. *(Photo courtesy Adam Coglianese)*

Trainer/owner Tim Snyder guides Lisa's Booby Trap back to the winner's circle while jockey Kent Desormeaux celebrates after winning the Loudonville Stakes at Saratoga. *(Photo courtesy Adam Coglianese)*

Tim Snyder shares a celebratory embrace with his mother-in-law, Carol Calley, near the winner's circle at Saratoga after they watched Lisa's Booby Trap remain undefeated with a victory in the Loudonville Stakes. *(Photo courtesy Adam Coglianese)*

Tim and Lisa's Booby Trap at the Calley farm in Camillus, New York. *(Photo courtesy Tim Snyder)*

Lisa's Booby Trap pokes her head out of the stall while resting at Finger Lakes. *(Photo courtesy Tim Snyder)*

Tim walks with Lisa after giving the filly a bath at Saratoga Race Course in the summer of 2010. *(Photo courtesy Tim Snyder)*

Jockey Kent Desormeaux rides Lisa's Booby Trap into the paddock at Saratoga before the Loudonville Stakes, while Tim Snyder walks alongside. *(Photo courtesy Tim Snyder)*.

Tim takes a nap with T-Bone, his Jack Russell terrier, at the Calley home in Camillus. *(Photo courtesy Tim Snyder)*

Tim Snyder preps Lisa's Booby Trap prior to the Riskaverse Stakes at Saratoga, on Sept. 2, 2010. It would be the first loss of Lisa's career. *(Photo courtesy Brien Bouyea)*

Lisa, in a full pre-race sweat, before finishing last in the Rachel Alexandra Stakes at Saratoga on August 1, 2011. *(Photo courtesy Brien Bouyea)*

Carol paused, her voice breaking at the memory.

"She was very devoted to me, more than I probably deserved. Even as a little kid . . . she always wanted to be around me. She thought a lot of me, and there are times when I wonder if I gave as much in return. I don't know. I feel guilty sometimes, and I don't even know why. But for her to tell me that—*I'm coming back as a horse*—it's unusual, right? For the longest time I didn't even think about it. I mean, those things don't happen."

Tim, ever the pragmatist, was even less prone to flights of fantasy. People died and then they were gone. Life went on. That much he had learned.

Yet there was something about Lisa that made him wonder whether it was just the meds talking, or her natural inclination to comfort those around her. What about that time at Beulah Park, when he and Lisa were standing in the paddock? She looked at the young apprentice getting a boot up into the saddle of one of their horses, and she swore to Tim that just for a moment she thought she saw something.

"A halo," Tim explained. "She said there was a halo above his head. I told her she was crazy. Figured it was just something to do with her seizures. But the next day, you know what happened? A horse stepped on the kid and killed him. Deader than shit. It was like she had a vision of some kind. Not like she predicted it or anything, but she saw . . . something."

Lisa Ann Calley died at home on December 24, 2003. Christmas Eve. She was thirty-seven years old. Five days later she was interred at Sacred Heart Cemetery in Lakeland, New York, just a few minutes' drive from her home and her horses.

Carol, thinking back to her daughter's tomboyish ways, and how she fidgeted anxiously throughout her first communion ceremony because she was so agitated by the dress she had been compelled to wear, decided to bury Lisa in slacks and a hooded shirt.

"I wanted her to be comfortable," Carol said with a laugh. "And I knew she wouldn't be comfortable in a dress."

Inscribed on the modest headstone at Lisa's gravesite are the following words: *"Weep not father and mother for me, for I am waiting in glory for thee."*

In the upper left corner, etched into the gray stone, is the image of a long-haired young woman standing in front of a racehorse, her hands gently clasping its muzzle. The animal is serene; the woman smiling, happy, healthy.

Chapter Eight

Grief is amorphous. It flows into your life, takes as much space as it needs, as much as it damn well pleases, filling every nook and cranny of your heart and soul, and then recedes an inch at a time. It's an illness of sorts, with no cure, no protocol for treatment, no assurance of a complete recovery. So who's to say that there is a right or wrong way to cope with it? Some people get on with their lives, finding comfort and solace in the routine of work or the support of family. Others slide into bed and try to sleep away the pain.

Tim Snyder hit the road, trying, as he had so many times in the past, to outrun the hurt.

It happened only a week or so after Lisa had died, a week in which Tim had stumbled quietly through the days, hardly talking to anyone, leaving the house for hours on end, returning late at night without explaining where he had been or what he was doing. Carol had known Tim long enough by now to understand the way he was, a hyperactive chatterbox who could weave a story across the space of an entire night when the mood struck him, but a man unlikely to share with anyone the enormity of a loss such as this. He would endure quietly, in solitude, comforting himself with time around the backstretch, the only place where he felt truly comfortable, and where nothing seemed to change. In time, she figured, he'd come around.

"I was in my own little world, too," Carol recalled of those first few days after Lisa's death. "And I guess I didn't realize how hard Timmy was taking it. He seemed okay. Then one morning I woke up, and he was just . . . gone. No goodbyes, no explanation, nothing. He just disappeared. That made me mad."

Imagine losing a daughter to cancer, and then losing the son-in-law you had welcomed into your home; the son-in-law you had embraced and supported and loved despite all his baggage and eccentricities. The Calley family had accepted Tim for who and what he was, without judging him or trying to remake him. It was reasonable, of course, to think that things might change now; that Tim would eventually move out of the house and begin to rebuild his life. That would only be normal. But surely they would play some role in the reconstruction. They were family now, bound perhaps not by blood, but by something equally profound.

How could he trample all over that? How could he just . . . leave?

Nearly a decade later, Tim squirmed uncomfortably at

the memory, and struggled to put into words the rationale for his sudden departure.

"I couldn't bear it," he said. "The thought of being here, in this house, without Lisa. I just couldn't do it. Every time I looked up I'd see the pictures on the wall. Her face was everywhere. Then I'd close my eyes and think about the last time I saw her, when they were putting her on a gurney and wheeling out of the house. I could see the hearse right outside the window, sitting in the driveway, getting ready to take her away. Long as I was here, living in this house, there was no escaping it. I couldn't sleep, I couldn't eat. I had to get away."

Carol and Frank didn't see it that way; neither did Tim's closest friend. Unlike the Calleys, though, John Tebbutt had seen this act before from Tim, the inability to cope with circumstances beyond his control, and the subsequent panic-stricken urge to flee. He understood Tim's weakness in these matters and the upbringing that had made him this way. So he wasn't completely shocked to hear that Tim was gone. But he also sympathized with the Calleys, who had now suffered a second loss. If the first one ripped their hearts out, this one pissed them off.

"They had great affection for him," Tebbutt said, "and they were upset when he left. It's like losing another kid, in a way. It was wrong of him to do that, but this all gets back to Timmy's basic personality—his rudeness and isolation. That's the way he deals with things. It's a coping mechanism, and not a very good one, at times. He didn't do well for a while after Lisa died. Quite a while, actually. I didn't even know he was gone, at first. I didn't hear from him for the longest time.

Then, after a few months, I got a call. And then more calls, every night for a week or more. Then they'd stop and I wouldn't hear anything for a few more months. And then he'd start calling again. I never knew what to expect—his mood would vary depending on the time of the day or night that he called, and how much drugs and alcohol he had in him."

Tebbutt would get no argument on that assessment from Tim, who by his own admission "kinda went nuts." He had gotten up before dawn one morning, while the house was still dark, tossed his clothes into a suitcase, jumped into his truck (he left the horse trailer behind), and pointed the nose west.

"Drove straight across the country," Tim said. "Didn't sleep at all. Shit, I didn't sleep much for the next six months. I don't remember much about the trip, except that I stopped somewhere in Indiana to call my sister. Told her I was coming to California."

Cheryl was neither surprised to get the phone call nor reluctant to open her home; she had provided an oasis for her little brother before, and she would willingly do it again. As with most encounters in Tim's life, there were no parameters to define this one, no timetable for arriving or leaving. He would show up one day, stay as long as he liked, and then move on. Same as always.

"He was completely lost when he got out here," Cheryl said. "I think he was depressed and in a terrible emotional state for at least two or three years. I mean, he stayed here for two years, then left, but he still wasn't right. And he was sick a lot of the time, too. He hadn't been taking care of himself and his stomach was all bloated and distended. I was worried about him. Timmy had a life, a business, a partner. He and Lisa did hard work, and they did it together. Suddenly his partner was gone and he had to start all over again. By himself."

By himself.

That's the part that baffled and wounded the Calley family. Why did he have to do anything on his own? Weren't they still part of his life, his family?

"There were a lot of hard feelings among them after Tim left," observed Cheryl. "They were all under such tremendous stress during those last few months, when Lisa was so sick. That can happen in any family. But after she died, and Tim just took off . . . well, they weren't too happy about that. He came out here and he didn't go back, which really hurt Carol. She and Tim have a very special relationship. It's unique. Totally platonic, but not like a normal mother-in-law and son-in-law relationship. It's wonderful and special, and he betrayed that by leaving. But you have to understand—that's what Tim does, because that's the behavior that was modeled for him when he was growing up. He doesn't know any other way."

For the first month or so he did nothing, just sat around and licked his wounds. He stared at the walls, watched a lot of television, avoided sleep for fear of the dreams that he'd have, dreams in which Lisa would appear to him, which was at once reassuring and gut-wrenching, for eventually the dream would end and he'd wake up, bathed in sweat, wanting to cry.

"I guess you'd call it a breakdown," Tim said. "It was like I was living a bad goddamn movie that wouldn't end. It played over and over. I kept waiting for it to stop. A lot of crazy shit went through my mind—sometimes I thought about killing myself."

Tim said his drinking was only sporadic, but what the episodes lacked in frequency, they more than made up for with intensity.

"I went off a few times," he acknowledged. "Crack-ups, tantrums—whatever you want to call them. I almost tore my sister's house apart a couple times. But she let me stay, of course, even if it meant she had to get out for a while. I thought her husband was a lazy-ass shit, didn't work, and yet he used to bully my sister around. One day I just had enough of his shit, so I took a cane and broke his nose, told him I'd kill him if he ever hurt my sister again. She was mad at both of us, so she left for a while. Came back eventually, though. Told me I needed to get some help. She was probably right, but I never did see a psychiatrist. I'm not big on that stuff. Not big on doctors, either."

Inertia, he told himself. That would do the trick. If only he could keep moving, stay busy, occupy his body with so much work that he'd be too exhausted to think about the past. That was the key: get up every morning, put both feet on the floor, and go to work.

He started out doing odd jobs on his sister's house, helping to fix things up. Then he bought some equipment and began power-washing houses. He detailed cars. It was simple, mindless work. Drudgery, really, but at least it filled the days with a sense of productivity. At least it put some change in his pocket, which, given the fact that Tim was basically broke, wasn't such a bad thing. For a while he had no interest in resurrecting any sort of career that revolved around horses, despite the fact that horses were all he really knew. Being around them would be too painful; they would remind him of Lisa, and of a better time.

One day, though, he drove over to Del Mar Racetrack. He watched a couple races, dropped a few bucks, and by the end of the day felt something stirring in his belly. Not long after that he stopped by the track again, and this time he roamed the backstretch. Tim had been away from the business for a while, and it had been many years since he'd worked in California, but he still had contacts, he still had experience, and he figured maybe it was time to put those things to work.

"I started driving a horse van again," Tim said. "Easy money. I could do it in my sleep."

He paused, chuckled.

"Practically did, a few times."

One of the good things about driving a truck is that you have plenty of time to think, and to get things straight in your head. Of course, that's the bad thing, as well. There was, for example, the day that Tim was driving a van filled with six-figure show horses from Los Angeles International Airport to an event in Indio, California, when his mind began to drift.

"I was going down the interstate, and I just started thinking about Lisa," he remembered. "Next thing I knew, the brakes are locked up and I'm sliding off the road with six horses in the back. That was a damn close call. Could have been killed because I wasn't paying attention. So I finished the trip, unloaded the horses, got my check, parked the van, and I quit. For a while, anyway. I still wasn't mentally right to drive a horse van."

He went back to power washing and detailing cars, did what he could to make ends meet, so that he wouldn't have to depend on his sister. A car accident resulted in a modest cash settlement that temporarily boosted his savings account and allowed him to pay off some debt. Slowly, over time, he began to emerge from the darkness of depression. In the late winter of 2006, tired of California and itching to get back into the racing game, Tim packed up the used BMW he'd bought with his settlement money (his truck had died with a couple hundred thousand miles on the odometer), and headed for home.

But where exactly was that?

Tim had no answer, so he did what he'd always done: he drifted. From California to Arizona, then north to Oregon and Washington, stopping to see one of his brothers along the way. One morning, after sleeping in his car near the border of Montana and Wyoming, he stopped at a convenience store to use a pay phone. His first and only call was to Carol Calley, with whom he had not spoken in two years.

"I'm dead-flat broke," Tim told her. "I've been siphoning gas to run the car. And you know what? There's too many prisons around here. I keep this up, I'm gonna end up in one of them."

He paused.

"Can you send me some money? I'm on my way to see you."

Carol thought for a moment, letting silence fill the line.

Do I really want to do this?

Truth be told, she was still angry with him, still hurt and offended by the way he had run off. Nevertheless, this was her son-in-law on the other end of the phone. Lisa's husband, the man to whom she'd been married for nearly nine years. He needed help. He wanted to come home.

How could she say no?

The next day Tim picked up a wire transfer in Wyoming. He filled the car with gas, got himself something to eat, and started driving. It took him a while to get there, as he meandered around the country, driving south through Louisiana and Florida before heading back up the Eastern Seaboard. Along the way he would check in periodically with Carol and Frank, just to see how they were doing and to assure them that he was on his way.

Then, one day, he simply showed up on the doorstep of their house in Camillus; the very same house where he and Lisa had lived, and where Lisa had died. He and Carol talked for a while, the conversation at first stilted and then gradually more comfortable. Carol asked if he needed a place to stay. Tim said that he did. Maybe they could work something out? Tim had always been handy. The Calleys had an older home, a fair amount of property that needed tending. Tim could help them. In return, they would give him a room.

It seemed to make sense.

"He moved right back in," Carol said. "I know some people think that's kind of odd, but we were glad to see him. We missed him. And he had nowhere else to go."

Before settling in, Tim wanted to take care of something important. He had left abruptly in the winter months more than two years earlier, before the headstone had been placed on Lisa's burial site. He'd heard from Carol that it was beautiful, the image of Lisa with one of her winning horses, culled from a photo taken in the winner's circle at Finger Lakes some years earlier. He wanted to see it for himself, so he drove to

Sacred Heart and knelt near the stone. He whispered to Lisa, told her how much he missed her, and how he had come back home. He hoped she would understand.

"I needed some closure on the cemetery and the grave," Tim explained. "That's part of the reason I came back. And I wanted to see my family. What can I tell you? I left on the run, and it took me some time to get my shit together."

Chapter Nine

OCALA, FLORIDA
JANUARY 8, 2010

At some point in the previous few days he'd already made up his mind. He had two thousand dollars to his name, every wrinkled bill stuffed into his boot to prevent anyone from stealing it, and now he was about to give it up willingly in exchange for a horse of modest pedigree and questionable ability. If anyone had suggested to Tim Snyder that he was out of his mind, they wouldn't have gotten much of an argument—not even from Snyder himself.

Tim had spent the better part of three years trying to put his life back together, but he had precious little to show for it. He had worked primarily for his buddy John Tebbutt, galloping horses and assisting with training duties at Tebbutt's barn at Finger Lakes Racetrack, but it was sporadic work made even less lucrative by the fact that Tim would sometimes disappear for days or weeks on end. Whenever he came around, though, there was a job waiting, and that, combined with the fact that he had a roof over his head in Camillus, thanks to the generosity of the Calley family, lent some stability to Tim's otherwise chaotic life.

Tebbutt had decided in December 2009 that he would spend the winter in Florida, setting up a small operation (approximately a half dozen horses) at a training center in Delray Beach and shipping horses to Gulfstream on race days. He offered Tim a job for the duration.

"John is a friend," Tim said. "We've had our differences over the years, but he's always had work for me. He's a good guy. He'd always wanted to spend the winter in Florida, and this seemed like a good time to do it. I was his main man, galloping horses, getting them ready to race. It was an all-day job."

Tebbutt knew that money was a significant problem for Tim; he also knew that while his friend was a highly competent horseman who would never have trouble getting backstretch work, Tim missed both the excitement and opportunity that came with being an owner. He was fifty-six years old, virtually broke, and had nothing to show for his nearly four decades in the business. He had a home, but no house; he had an empty bank account. His assets, beyond the two grand in cash, were limited to a beat-up station wagon and a feisty little Jack Russell terrier named T-Bone.

"He was in a tough situation," Tebbutt recalled. "I told him the best way to get out of debt and get a leg up on the whole situation was to get himself a horse, get back in the game, start churning them again."

It wasn't like Tim required much in the way of persuasion. He wanted a horse of his own, even if his plan was simply to sell the nag for a small profit shortly after it came into his possession. He and Lisa had made a living doing precisely that; why couldn't he do it again . . . on his own?

So Tim began poking around, making phone calls, looking for a horse that would fit into his meager budget. Tebbutt made inquiries on his behalf, as well, eventually leading to a conversation with Don Hunt, an owner and broker who had a farm in Ocala. Hunt had plenty of stock, some of it in Snyder's price range. He also had something of a history with Tim, the two having done business on numerous occasions over the years, some of it collegial, some of it acrimonious.

The most noteworthy transaction was actually one of the smallest, but resulted in a significant amount of confusion and a whopping inconvenience for Tim. It happened in 2003, while Lisa was battling cancer and Tim was trying to pay bills by hauling horses up and down the East Coast. According to Tim, Hunt had authorized Snyder to take permanent possession of a horse that he was transporting to another owner, an acquaintance of Hunt's. Tim had the horse for only a short time before selling it. The horse, Halo's Wish, went on to hit the board a few times, resulting in a dispute over ownership. Since Snyder had taken possession through informal channels, he had no documentation on the horse and thus no proof of ownership. In the summer of 2003 a ruling of indefinite suspension was handed down by stewards at Finger Lakes. The sanction would effectively prevent Tim from owning or training horses at any track in North America for nearly four years, until the suspension was lifted in May 2007.

"It was ridiculous. I didn't steal a horse," Tim said. "The

horse was given to me, but then it wins some money and suddenly everybody wants a piece of it. I didn't even care at the time. My wife was dying. But that cost me four years. Eventually Don called the stewards and got everything straightened out."

While not addressing the specifics of the incident, Hunt did offer this assessment of Snyder:

"Tim is different, that's for sure. I like him, we're friends, and I've sold him a number of horses over the years. But he will say things he should not say at times. And he's got a little bit of larceny in him."

Regardless of any ill feelings the two may have had toward one another, they were prepared to do business once again in early 2010. During the course of a phone conversation, Hunt told Tim about a horse he might like, a big bay filly, three years old, that had the lines and musculature of a serious racehorse, but had thus far been disinclined to run so much as a step. Maybe Timmy could take a look at her. After all, he needed a project.

Details of the initial offer are steeped in murkiness, and vary by small degrees depending on the source. According to Snyder, Hunt wanted $4,500 for the unnamed filly. Snyder told him he had only two thousand dollars to his name. Would Hunt consider accepting the two grand as a down payment, with the remaining $2,500 to be paid out of the horse's winnings?

"Don said she was a maiden filly out of a stakes-winning mare," Tim explained. "A real good-looking horse, but she was blind in one eye and there had been some trouble with her feet. Other than that, she was in good shape. I didn't care. I was used to working with horses like that. I know Donny got insulted later because he thought I claimed that he sold me a bad horse, or that the horse wasn't taken care of. I didn't mean to imply that. She was a great horse. If she had any problems, she was born with them. I said I wanted to take a look at the horse, and if I liked what I saw, I'd give him whatever money I had."

Hunt would later intimate that the agreed-upon sale price was in excess of $4,500, but added, "If that's what Timmy wants to say, let him stick with it. Timmy has said a lot of things to make this story better than it really is. I'll go along with whatever Tim wants to say, except the part about the horse being crippled and a piece of crap when he picked her up. That is absolutely not true. The horse weas drop-dead gorgeous."

Around this same time, the horse broker John Shaw got a telephone call from Hunt, alerting him to the possibility of a buyer for that filly they had exchanged a couple months earlier, the one slow enough to be timed with a sundial. The numbers were small, but that didn't concern Shaw. Any return on the investment was acceptable at this point.

"Don told me he had a guy at Finger Lakes who wanted to buy the horse," Shaw recalled. "That guy was Snyder. I'd get twelve hundred dollars now, and twelve hundred when the horse won its first race. I guess Don was going to give me half, and he would take the other half. I didn't care. He asked if I was happy with the deal and I said, 'Sure, it's fine. But trust me, there won't ever be any more money, because this horse is never going to win a race.'"

The deal would not close until Tim arrived in Ocala and got the opportunity to run his hands over the horse himself, and to look her dead in the eye (both the good one and the bad one); or so he said, anyway. In reality, he'd already come to a decision by the time he got behind the wheel of the Dodge pickup truck that he'd he borrowed from Tebbutt. (He'd also borrowed Tebbutt's credit card, since he had no cash beyond that which was stuffed into his boot, and the truck would need gas, and both the driver and its cargo would need food.)

"I knew Timmy was talking with Don about buying a horse," Tebbutt said. "One day he walked into the barn and said, 'I need to pick up my horse.' I said, 'Okay, take the truck and trailer. Spend the night down there. Relax. Take your time with it.'"

Tebbutt laughed.

"He left at two in the afternoon, got back by two in the morning. Twelve hours, round trip. Made it to work the next morning with a new horse. A big, new horse, kind of crooked, but pretty."

It was a whirlwind of a trip because Tim, impulsive by nature, saw no reason to extend the process beyond a single day. He liked the horse and wanted to get to work with her.

"Took me five hours to drive up," he said, recounting the itinerary. "When I got there, Don was waiting. Basically he said, 'This is the horse. You want her, she's yours. Just make it quick. I gotta get out of town.' I had intentions of taking her regardless, but I never pulled the money out of my boot till I got a good look at her. She was seventeen hands high, just beautiful, and based on that alone I wanted her. I saw the spot on her eye, and she was a little off, structurally. I didn't care.

Shit, I'm not thinking then that I'll ever take her to Saratoga. I'm thinking I'll take her to Finger Lakes, where maybe she can win a race or two. Cheap track, cheap races. I don't think she's nothing special, just a big horse that'll get me started. So I gave Don two thousand in cash, he gave me the papers, we shook hands, and off I went. Stopped at the Waffle House for a sandwich and a cup of coffee, then drove straight back to Delray."

Within just a few days, the strain of being a new owner (and a penniless one, at that), combined with the burden of his day job, began to wear on Tim's prickly personality. One morning he got into a disagreement with a younger worker over access to the barn's laundry facility. It was a silly argument—Tim chewing out the kid because he was always monopolizing the washing machine, filling the room with horse bandages, cluttering things up. Really, though, it was just Tim blowing off steam as he did periodically, especially when the pressure in his life mounted.

Tebbutt, accustomed to his friend's occasional outbursts, tried to diffuse the situation—*Timmy, come on, give the kid a break; he's just trying to do his job*—which Tim interpreted not merely as benign diplomatic posturing, but a significant act of betrayal. He cursed at the kid, cursed at Tebbutt, threw a saddle down the shedrow, told them all to go fuck themselves, and stormed out of the barn, vowing never to return.

"He had a meltdown," Tebbutt recalled with a laugh. "It's not like it hadn't happened before."

Tim agreed.

"Yeah, I quit," he said. "Hell, I quit John a half dozen times at least. I was just so burned out and tired. All that galloping, training, riding. I was doing everything. And now I had a horse of my own. It was too much. By this point I hadn't even done anything with the horse, maybe a little jog, put the tack on her. But that's it. I knew she needed work, I was worried about the bills, and I was disgusted with my job. I was totally worn out and too tired to even take care of my own horse. I don't like cheating on a horse. When you start cheating on your horse for someone else's horse, you're in trouble. So I had a blowup and said, 'See you later.'"

As for the new horse in the barn . . .

"You take her," Tim told Tebbutt as he walked away. "She's all yours."

Tebbutt just shrugged. He'd seen this act before and knew Tim would come around eventually. So he cared for the horse for more than a week, in anticipation of the inevitable phone call. When it came, Tim informed Tebbutt that he had moved to Ocala, where he was working for another Finger Lakes–based trainer name Dave Markgraf.

"He had about fifty head in Ocala," Snyder said of Markgraf. "His main exercise boy had just gone to jail on a DWI, so he needed someone right away, and I needed the money. He gave me five hundred bucks cash to get started and I went to work the next morning. Then it turned out the kid was on his third DWI, so he wasn't getting out of jail anytime soon, and they asked me to stay on for a while. They told me I could ship my horse up from Delray, and they'd give me a stall for her as long as I was working there. I did him a favor by training his horses in a pinch; he did me a favor by giving me free stall space."

So, less than two weeks after she had arrived at Tebbutt's barn, the filly was on her way back to Ocala.

"I had no idea what to make of her when she left," Tebbutt said. "I wasn't even sure I'd ever see her again. She was Timmy's horse, and all she'd done was walk along the shedrow. She was way out of balance—her feet needed more work—but she was so big and strong. Timmy's a good horseman—I figured he'd get her to the races eventually. At that level, if you can break your maiden, win forty-five hundred bucks, then turn around and sell the horse, you've done okay. She seemed like that kind of horse."

Whatever kind of horse she was, or would become, she very nearly did it under the guidance of another owner and trainer. If not for Tim's eruption and subsequent departure, he might well have surrendered possession of the filly in a more permanent manner. You see, ironically, Tim's volatile nature, which had caused him so many problems in the past, may have prevented him from parting ways with the horse before ever finding out how talented she really was.

Not more than a couple days after Tim left for Ocala, two young men showed up at the Delray Training Center, flush with money and a new truck, and an empty trailer in need of cargo. They stopped by Tebbutt's barn and became smitten with the big unnamed filly.

"How much?" they asked.

Tebbutt shrugged, explained that the horse wasn't for sale, and that he wasn't even the owner—though he certainly could have claimed otherwise, given the circumstances of Snyder's departure. After all, Tim had told him to keep the filly.

The two young men persisted, said they would consider going as high as fifteen thousand dollars. They asked if they could take the filly out of her stall, watch her walk around a bit. Tebbutt did not waver. For that, Tim Snyder will be forever grateful.

"I missed that boat, fortunately," Tim would later acknowledge. "If I'd been there, I might have sold her. I had no attachment to her at all. I was in Ocala, my horse was up near Miami. I was broke and kicking myself for buying a horse. I was living in my car, didn't even have money for gas. That's how things were going. If I'd known that I could have maybe quadrupled my investment? I'd have gotten rid of her."

In the meantime, there was the issue of providing the filly with a proper name; given that she was now officially a three-year-old, this part of the process was long overdue. Then again, it was the fate of horses deemed ill-suited to the track to linger in limbo for months if not years, awaiting the care of an owner who had sufficient confidence in the animal to invest in the accoutrements of training, which included registering the horse's official moniker with The Jockey Club.

The naming of thoroughbred racehorses is a process steeped in tradition and protocol. Typically, an owner will choose a name that pays homage to the foal's lineage (if the bloodline is worth noting) while perhaps reflecting its individuality—something about its owner, perhaps, or its appearance. Thus, the son of Bold Bidder is named Spectacular Bid; the offspring of Fool-Me-Not and What a Pleasure is named Foolish Pleasure.

At the lower end of the sport, where breeding is more muddled and purchase prices significantly lower, owners are less inclined to remain tethered to tradition. In much the same way that a family pet might be identified, forty-five-hundred-dollar race horses are often named through a combination of whimsy and hunch.

And so, improbably enough, the bay filly out of Drewman and Ennuhway became . . .

Lisa's Booby Trap.

Here is where the story takes a decidedly unromantic turn. But Snyder is nothing if not honest, and he tells the tale of Lisa's Booby Trap without a hint of regret or apology. A widower rebounding from years of grief and loneliness—a widower who has lived most of his life in the margins of society—does what he can to get through the day. Sometimes, in the case of Tim Snyder, that meant hanging out at a South Florida gentlemen's club with a cringe-inducing name: The Booby Trap, which catered to the racing crowd at nearby Calder Racetrack, where Tim and John Tebbutt were sometimes visitors.

"It was right down the street," Snyder said of the club. "We'd go to Calder maybe twice a week to visit the tack shop, and then we'd go to The Booby Trap. If you were one of the track guys, all you had to do was stop in and take a seat at the bar, and they'd give you a sandwich—roast beef, pastrami . . . whatever. Sandwiches so big and sloppy you couldn't eat the whole thing. With fries and cole slaw. We could eat practically for free—just had to throw the girls a few bucks every once in a while."

Snyder shrugged. "Some people don't like that part of the story. What am I supposed to do—lie?"

Added John Tebbutt: "Everybody gets lonely. It's not a

crime. And anyway, they had a free lunch at The Booby Trap, the lunches were delicious, and two out of three girls were cute."

Tebbutt laughed.

"Of course, the third one you'd kind of have to put your sandwich down and leave. But we spent some time there. Nothing wrong with that."

In the beginning, Tim wryly tried to name his new horse solely after the club; upon discovering that "Booby Trap" had already been registered with the Jockey Club, he added "Lisa" to the front. Thus was born Lisa's Booby Trap. If anyone is offended by that juxtaposition, well . . . rest assured that Snyder's wife would have gotten the joke.

"Wouldn't have bothered her in the least," Tebbutt said.

Tebbutt actually wasn't involved in the naming of the horse. He and Tim had discussed various options, but then Tim bolted for Ocala, and the filly soon followed, leaving Tebbutt in the dark. It was while in Ocala that a bit of research revealed the disappointing news that Booby Trap had already been taken, leaving Tim scratching his head for a suitable name. Stumped, he began soliciting suggestions. His in-laws recommended naming the filly after their daughter. She loved horses, after all, and wouldn't this be a good way to honor her memory.

"How about Lisa's Pride?" Carol offered.

"Ah, I don't know," Tim responded. "Maybe."

He thought about naming the horse after his daughter or grandson, but for some reason discarded those options, as well. It was almost as though he didn't want to burden the horse with a name that might provoke any sort of reverence or expectation. In all likelihood the filly would meet the fate of just about every other horse he'd owned: it would run a few times, maybe hit the board, maybe not, and be passed on to someone else. You name a horse after one of your grandkids, or your beloved deceased wife, and you're sort of obligated to hang onto it for a while.

Tim liked the looks of the filly. He thought she had some potential. But he was hardly in love with the horse. It wasn't his nature to allow such connections to distract him from the job at hand. Under the circumstances, a more frivolous or irreverent name seemed appropriate. So Tim settled on Lisa's Booby Trap, a choice that was, not surprisingly, available for the taking, according to Jockey Club records. He paid the seventy-five-dollar registration fee and went back to work. It wasn't until some two months later, when he returned to New York, that Tim introduced the filly to his in-laws.

"Frank, Carol . . . I'd like you to meet Lisa's Booby Trap."

They were not amused.

"My husband was a little upset," Carol said. "I wasn't really mad, but I did think it was kind of odd. I guess it works, though. I mean, that's Timmy."

It's Carol Calley's nature to be diplomatic and nonconfrontational. She is, by all accounts, a sweet-tempered, patient, and generous woman. So her recollection of the story, according to Tim, is somewhat suspect.

"They hated the name," Tim said. "Just hated it. And my father-in-law was real mad about it for a while."

Well, who could blame him? Really—who names a horse after his dead wife and . . . *a strip club*?

"Look, I liked the strip joint, and the strip joint's name

was taken," Tim argued logically, if not altogether convincingly. "So I put my wife's name in front of it. I agree that Booby Trap is a very tricky name. But I figured most people wouldn't even know what it meant."

Nor would they have a chance to pass judgment since, in all likelihood, the horse would never amount to anything more than a Finger Lakes claimer. Tim insists that it never once occurred to him that combining "Lisa" with "Bobby Trap" might be construed as disrespectful to the memory of his wife. In retrospect, he can see how others might have viewed it that way.

He also doesn't give a shit.

"How she got her name is the truth," Tim said. "I'm not fabricating anything, I'm not trying to justify anything. It's my business, my horse, my wife who died. That's the way I named her, that's what I wanted. I wasn't going to adjust the name for anyone else."

In the coming months, as the saga of Lisa's Booby Trap went national, writers and broadcasters would fumble awkwardly for the right words as they struggled to project just the right combination of romance and fantasy the story seemed to entail, if not demand. More often than not, they would fail utterly, for how could they tug cheaply at the heartstrings while describing the exploits of a grieving trainer who combined the names of his dead wife and his favorite strip joint when christening his new horse?

It boggled the mind as it taxed the dexterity of sportswriters across the land. Some chose to simply ignore the less savory aspects of the story. For example, the esteemed *Blood-Horse* magazine said this about Lisa's Booby Trap in the summer of 2010: "The 3-year-old filly is trained and owned by Timothy Snyder, who named her for his wife who died of cancer in 2003."

True enough . . . but not exactly accurate. Of course, those who strove for accuracy risked jarring juxtaposition at the least, unintentional dark humor at the worst. From the *Daily Racing Form*: "Lisa's Booby Trap was named by Snyder for his wife Lisa, who died of [cervical] cancer in 2003, and for a gentlemen's club, The Booby Trap that he used to frequent in south Florida."

What?

A cathartic story should be neatly wrapped and presented, uncluttered by complications of the heart and the vagaries of life. Ideally, it should be a Hallmark card: you open it up, let the sentimentality wash over you, have a good cry, and forget about it almost instantly.

The story of Lisa's Booby Trap could not easily be shoehorned into this classification, but that didn't stop people from trying. And the very fact that it was more complicated, more interesting, and ultimately more *human* provoked a broad range of reactions—from confusion to bemusement to outright anger. This was particularly true among those who for one reason or another—personal conflicts, jealousy, a tumultuous business history—were not fans of Tim Snyder.

"He's a strange guy," said John Shaw. "I mean, anybody who names a horse after a strip club . . . and then you hear him talk . . . Donny [Hunt] tells me the story, and he said Snyder only named it Lisa because he figured if he named it after his wife, that his mother-in-law would chip in some money toward the horse."

As for Don Hunt, he too is somewhat skeptical about the story. But then, for all the dewy romanticism associated with their sport, horsemen can be a crusty, cynical lot.

"Tim's wife was a nice person," Hunt said. "I liked her. She was a hard worker. But they struggled when they were together. I think people are making more out of this than they should."

As for the name?

"Believe me, anybody else you'd scratch your head," Hunt observed. "With Tim . . . it sort of fits."

Even those who know Tim best found his choice of names quizzical, although not out of character. But they are fiercely defensive of his relationship with Lisa, as well as the success he would ultimately find with the horse that bore her name. It is also true that some of them, including his mother-in-law and sister, provided financial assistance to Tim while he was in Florida in the weeks and month shortly after he purchased the filly who would become Lisa's Booby Trap. Like John Tebbutt, they know Tim well, and they begrudge him nothing.

"Some people don't understand Tim or why he named this horse the way he did," Cheryl Hall explained. "That's because they grew up in a normal household."

Neither Tim nor Cheryl had that luxury, so when he called his sister and explained that he would not be choosing some genteel, faux-bourgeois name for his new filly, nor a simple, elegant name intended only to honor some family member, she was not surprised.

"I got the name," Tim told her.

"Oh, yeah? What is it?"

"Lisa's Booby Trap!"

At first, Cheryl didn't know what to make of the name.

"Obviously I understood the first part," she recalled. "Lisa was his wife. That part was good. But then he told me about The Booby Trap, and how it was this place where he went for lunch. I thought it was silly, but harmless. To be honest with you, I think he went there more for the lunch than the boobies. Tim is not a guy who frequented strip joints his whole life; he's a guy who knew how to find a free meal. And you have to understand—to a guy like Tim, it wouldn't matter if he named the horse after a church or a titty bar. No difference. He's accepting of all things. He also truly does not give a crap what people think."

Although John Tebbutt's midday excursions to The Booby Trap with Tim partially inspired the horse's new name, it wasn't until a few months later, when Tim showed up at Finger Lakes, that Tebbutt learned exactly what had happened.

"I thought it was a great name," he said. "A little odd, yeah, but funny. And exactly the kind of thing Tim would do. Of course, when I told my wife about it, she said, 'If you ever do that to me I'll come back from the grave and kill you.'"

It was at Finger Lakes that Tebbutt fully reconnected with his old friend, whose journey from Florida, with new horse in tow, had been more than a little rocky.

"In March, about a month before I came back north, a horse flipped over on me at the barn," Tim said. "At first they thought I was having a heart attack—it hurt that bad. Took them fifteen minutes to get me off the ground. Turned out

I got a swollen liver and three broken ribs, and no insurance to cover it. Man, I was sick."

At the time Snyder was living out of his car, with T-Bone as his constant companion (and if ever a dog seemed a perfect match for its owner, this was it). While recuperating he managed to secure the use of a trailer, provided by his employer, but for the better part of three weeks he could barely get out of bed.

"I was totally laid up. Never did see a doctor, just sweated it out," Tim said. "But I still took care of my horse. Had a young Mexican exercise rider who helped me out. That kid was a lifesaver. I don't even know his name. I think it was Jesus—that week, anyway. A lot of those kids are amazing. First thing they do when they get to this country is learn how to ride. They're small and ambitious and they ain't afraid to work. They're tough as hell and they can survive on practically nothing. I didn't have much money, but I paid him what I could."

Whatever Tim had left by the time he recovered, it wasn't enough to cover the costs of feeding and caring for a new thoroughbred racehorse, and for shipping that horse from Florida to New York. So he borrowed some money from his mother-in-law and he borrowed money from his sister, and he worked a deal with Markgraf in which the owner would ship Lisa's Booby Trap to Finger Lakes along with the rest of his stock, with the understanding that Tim would eventually pay him back.

Then he slid behind the wheel of his Ford Taurus, cupped a hand under his aching ribs, put T-Bone in the seat beside him, and chased the horse van up I-95 for twenty-four hours straight. They arrived in upstate New York in early April, the busted owner with a single horse and a hungry dog, and a mounting pile of debt.

Chapter Ten

When she arrived at Finger Lakes Racetrack in April 2010, Lisa's Booby Trap was just another cheap and obscure filly lazily munching hay in a stall, with virtually no reasonable chance of ever becoming anything more than that. She was prettier than most of her stablemates, taller, a bit gangly, but with long muscles still in development, and so she certainly looked like more of a racehorse. But appearances can be deceptive and breeding unreliable; no one knew better than Tim Snyder that the filly was far from the second coming of Ruffian. His goals for her remained modest: to correct any lingering structural issues and determine whether she was even capable of running. If he succeeded at that, then perhaps she might eventually make a few bucks at the track.

It remained, however, a daunting project.

Tim had started working with Lisa in Ocala, and what he saw both encouraged and distressed him. The fact that she was at least partially blind in one eye did not overly concern Snyder, for she did not seem distracted or hampered by it. One-eyed horses, or at least horses with diminished vision, routinely make it to the starting gate; some perform surprisingly well. Tim was confident that Lisa's Booby Trap fell into the latter category. When he approached from the blind side, Lisa would not spook easily, as some vision-impaired horses do. In a bridle, she did not jerk her head awkwardly, as if trying to accommodate the disability. She simply went about her business, almost as if the problem didn't exist.

"The eye was no big deal," Tim said. "I've been around a lot of blind horses. It doesn't stop them from running—if they want to run, they can run with a bad eye. That was the least of her problems."

A horse's genetic blueprint is determined very early in the game, and there is only so much that can be done after the fact to correct mistakes or shortcomings. It's best to concentrate on the things that can be fixed. In the case of Lisa's Booby Trap, that meant working on feet that were not designed for running. Like Don Hunt before him, Snyder recognized issues with Lisa's feet and attempted to correct them by trial and error.

"I trimmed her feet and put shoes on her when I first got her in Florida," Tim said. "Then I went to Ocala, and a month later I took some more off her feet, put another set of shoes on her. I was lucky to have a couple good blacksmiths who could help me. I've been lucky a lot with this horse. Seemed like everywhere I went, I knew somebody who needed me to work, and I needed their help, and we were able to work out a deal. You can't do it alone."

The way Tim saw it, maybe Lisa wasn't really the slowest horse in the world. Maybe she was simply a horse whose structural and balance issues were so severe that she was disinclined to even take that first step, for she knew what lay ahead: discomfort and anxiety. Imagine trying to run with one bare foot and one protected by a shoe. Imagine trying to run on shoes of unequal size. Imagine having legs of unequal length.

While none of these scenarios reflect exactly the issues faced by Lisa's Booby Trap, they offer a glimpse into the challenges encountered by anyone trying to prepare her for a career on the racetrack. The more Snyder worked with Lisa, the more he began to think that her feet were the source of all problems. She had a clubfoot on the right front side; on the left front, a diminished heel.

"So she's up on her heel on one side, and flat-footed on the other," Tim said. "It's like she's a got a high heel on one side, and a sneaker on the other. No way you can even walk like that, let alone run. It was very bad. Horses like that don't often make it to the racetrack; sometimes they do. Trainers don't notice that shit, usually, but it was really obvious with Lisa. That's why I ended up with her. Her lineage was fine, but she was structurally unsound. Trainers and owners get rid of horses in that condition, pawn them off. Usually, best a horse like that can hope for is to become a barn pony or a jumper. Basically a big pet. Nothing wrong with that. But I thought maybe Lisa could be more. I took her because she was big and had a long stride on her. She was graceful despite her problems."

Had Lisa's Booby Trap never stood in a starting gate, had she never become anything more than a cheap Finger Lakes claimer, chances are no one would have disputed Snyder's assertions about the condition of the horse, or the amount of work he put into her. As it happened, though, Lisa entered the spotlight just long enough for Snyder's claims to come into question.

"She was in bad shape when I got her," said Don Hunt. "Her feet were atrocious. I still have the X-rays to document the feet when I got her. But Tim did not do any miracle work with her feet. I did whatever straightening out there was, and apparently it did help the horse somewhat. She looked like a million bucks when they took her out of here. There wasn't any second-guessing about what she looked like. The horse was picture perfect when Tim bought her. I've got vet reports about how good her feet were."

John Shaw is similarly unconvinced that Snyder worked any magic with Lisa's Booby Trap.

"When I got her she looked fabulous, and Don takes great care of his horses, too. I read somewhere that Snyder said she was wormy or whatever. That's just hocus-pocus to make himself look better."

As for whether the filly's feet were as bad as Snyder claimed?

"I don't think she had a clubfoot" Shaw said. "If she has one now it's from poor shoeing. If she did have a clubfoot, it might have been just a little narrow. Don X-rayed her feet because she had some rotation on the coffin bone, which would cause her to be sore. And that's what basically turned it around, because he told Snyder to be aware of the possibility that she's got a rotation in the coffin bone. Other than that . . . I don't know."

Snyder gets visibly agitated when he hears this sort of thing. He claims that he never said anyone mistreated the filly; at the least, he never intended for that message to come across. But he stands by his assertion that the horse was a structural mess and that he put in the time to correct those issues—to the extent that they could be corrected.

"I changed the degree on her feet with every new shoeing," Tim said. "Her feet were way out in front of her, like having long nails. And each shoeing, I was getting her feet up underneath her, straight with the knee, so she wouldn't strain her tendons and ligaments. I'd cut the toe up, move the shoe back. But you can't make a drastic change; you have to do it a little at a time. It's a long, slow process."

John Tebbutt, a genial sort whose even temper serves as a neat counterbalance to Snyder's more volatile nature, bristles slightly when asked how much credit his friend deserves for the transformation of Lisa's Booby Trap.

"I think he deserves all the credit. After this horse started working well, everybody considered her a freak. When they are that far out of alignment you wonder how long they can last. It's like driving down the road with one good tire and three tires that are bald. It doesn't mean they can't run, it just usually means their time is very limited. And that turned out to be the case with Lisa. But in the beginning there was no reason to think she'd ever amount to anything. She was a big, good-looking horse, but her muscles didn't look right, and she was very awkward."

Tebbutt is at times almost oddly defensive about a man he openly describes as "a pain in the ass." But such is the nature of friendship, particularly when it has endured the twin tests of time and hardship.

"I have been Tim's best friend for a very long time," Tebbutt said. "That's not going to change, no matter what he does. "Since I quit drinking and drugging about fifteen years ago, I've become very compassionate to other people, you know? Tim has had a hard life. I try not to judge people in a negative way; I try to find the positives about them. Anybody that comes along, you try to support the best you can. I worked in California for a while, and I saw that from an old man I worked for. We were the first barn at Hollywood Park, and every single kind of person would come to his barn first, to borrow five dollars or fifty thousand. Or just to say hello. Everybody owed him a favor—from the chief stewards to the mega rich, to the hotwalker who never had anything and never would have anything. He was kind to everyone; that was an attribute I admired."

It's worth noting that the old man to whom Tebbutt referred was no ordinary backstretch plugger. His name was Charlie Whittingham, a Hall of Fame trainer widely regarded as one of the greatest horsemen in the game, as well as one of the most generous of spirit. With Whittingham as a mentor, it's probably no surprise that Tebbutt comes across as someone with unusual patience—at least where Tim Snyder is considered.

For example, when Tim returned to Finger Lakes from Ocala, he did so with the intent to continue working for Dave Markgraf. That arrangement lasted only a few days, and soon Tim found himself at Tebbutt's barn, in need of stall space, a job, a paycheck, and something else, as well.

He needed someone he could trust.

"I was the registered owner on Lisa, but I had no trainer's license," Snyder explained. "It had lapsed, and I didn't have the money to apply for a new one. You need six hundred bucks for the track fee, and another four-fifty for workman's comp, so that's a thousand bucks I didn't have at the time. I had already borrowed so much money to keep this horse going. I figured it made more sense to just run her in John's name. If she won a couple races, I could get my license and put her in my name."

For someone with Tim's naturally skeptical nature, the thought of turning over Lisa to another trainer, if only as a matter of protocol, was enough to cause a serious spike in anxiety.

"I didn't want to put the horse in anyone else's name, just in case she went the other way and turned out to be a nice horse," he said. "That could cause problems. Racing is a tough business; you've gotta watch your own ass."

Or have a friend willing to watch it for you. For Tim, that person was John Tebbutt, who became, in April 2010, the official trainer of Lisa's Booby Trap, and who saddled the horse in her first couple races—albeit with Tim, as an "assistant," right by his side.

"It wasn't a big deal," Tebbutt said with a shrug. "Just part of the game."

With the appropriate paperwork in place and his new

horse comfortably settling into her upstate home, Tim turned his attention to preparing Lisa for the racetrack. He continued to tinker with her feet and her shoes, until finally she appeared to walk normally, without bobbing from side to side. Then he went about the hard business of training, and correcting another of Lisa's apparent structural abnormalities: an imbalance in her shoulders.

Snyder first noticed the issue in Florida, when he worked Lisa in a eurociser. The eurociser is a circular, mechanized training apparatus, divided into stalls, that permits horses to walk or jog in a tightly controlled space, without having to bear the burden of a rider. Akin to a giant, horizontal hamster wheel, it's particularly useful when working with horses that are either new to the sport or recovering from some type of injury. In the case of Lisa's Booby Trap, it gave Tim Snyder an opportunity to monitor the gate and stride of his new filly; what he saw concerned him.

"Her right shoulder was much larger than her left shoulder," he recalled. "It was the strangest thing."

What Snyder quickly determined, after taking Lisa out on the track a few times, was that she was unable to switch leads while galloping. The concept of switching leads sounds complicated and mysterious to those who haven't spent any time around a racetrack (or around horses in general), but it's actually a normal and instinctive behavior, albeit one that sometimes needs tweaking and prodding. Basically, when a horse gallops it "leads" with the legs on one side of its body, meaning the legs on either the left or right side reach farther forward than the legs on the other side. (This contrasts with, say, a rabbit, which ambulates by pulling rear legs forward first, in tandem, and then front legs afterward.) If the horse leads with his left, he will first push off his right hind leg. Then he will reach forward simultaneously with his left hind leg and right foreleg. Finally, he pulls the left front leg forward. Then he repeats the motion, over and over, creating what appears to be a beautiful and effortless gallop. A horse leading with its right simply reverses the movement, driving first off its left rear leg.

When a horse runs in a straight line, it really doesn't matter whether a left or right lead is utilized. But it's generally accepted that when running in a circle, the inside leg should be the lead leg. In other words, a horse rounding the final turn of a racetrack, running in a counterclockwise direction, should be using its left—or inside—lead.

"If they're on the outside lead going through that turn, they can veer out fast and get into trouble," Snyder explained. "They have to be on the inside lead. Then, after they get through the turn, they switch to the outside lead because they want to go straight. Halfway down the stretch they'll switch again just because they're tired."

If the horse is sound and a natural runner—as all thoroughbred racehorses are presumed to be—all of this happens smoothly and imperceptibly. The jockey feels it, though, and sometimes can prompt the change in a horse that is either reluctant or too tired to think straight.

But when a horse fails to switch leads, it typically struggles and fades, for it is no longer running efficiently.

"If he's tired and he doesn't switch leads, something bad is going to happen," Snyder said. "He's going to fall or pull up, or veer out into traffic. Nothing good, that's for sure."

The first few times he galloped his new filly, Tim noticed that she would not use her left lead. Whether this was because of the imbalance in her shoulder muscles, or whether the failure to use the left lead caused the imbalance (or whether both were caused by her bad feet) was almost irrelevant. It was a serious impediment to her future as a racehorse, and it had to be corrected. Snyder wasn't sure how he was going to fix the problem, but he knew this much: he wanted it to remain a secret.

"I'd jog her all the way around to the backstretch, then only gallop a half-mile or so, because I knew people were watching. I didn't want all those big-time trainers and owners to see that she couldn't switch leads. Shit, some of these guys were paying a half-million dollars for horses that looked like jackasses. I had a horse that looked great, but didn't know how to run. I figured maybe if I could hide that fact for a little while, one of them would want her. Maybe they'd pay real money."

At the very least, Tim was encouraged by what he felt was a diagnostic breakthrough. Prior to being purchased by Snyder, the filly had routinely plodded through workouts of three-eighths of a mile in forty-three seconds, a good five to seven seconds slower than her peers. Thus the declaration by John Shaw (and others) that she was among the most hopeless of cases: a racehorse that would never race; a filly of almost incomprehensible torpor. Snyder saw and felt something else: a big, strong girl who wanted to run, but couldn't.

"She didn't know how to switch leads," he recalled. "I thought if I could get that worked out, maybe she'd be all right."

One day in late February, after a particularly energetic session of breezing, Snyder called his mother-in-law.

"If I can figure this out," he told her, "I think I might have one of the best horses on the East Coast."

Carol Calley didn't know how to respond. She was happy that Tim seemed excited, optimistic; she respected his knowledge of the game. Still . . .

One of the best horses on the East Coast?

Tim was prone to wild mood swings, ferocious highs and lows that knew no boundaries. He could be thrilled about a horse one day, moribund the next. Although she didn't say so at the time, Carol figured that eventually the filly would be revealed for what she was: a $4,500 gamble unlikely to ever pay off. But maybe that didn't really matter. If the horse never gave Tim a trip to the winner's circle, at least she'd rekindled his passion for horse racing, and maybe for life in general. In that sense, she'd been a solid investment.

Eventually, after a few weeks in upstate New York, Snyder noticed that Lisa tended to clip heels when she tried to switch leads. Once properly shod—and he stressed that this does not mean his previous owners failed her in this regard, but rather that more experimentation was necessary; in the case of Lisa's Booby Trap, this included the use of a rear shoe on a front foot—she was able to work crisply and efficiently, and before long she began to take on the appearance of a real racehorse.

Not that anyone really noticed. Finger Lakes is several hundred miles and a metaphorical galaxy away from the center of the racing universe. While the most notable performers in that season's three-year-old crop—Super Saver, Lookin' at Lucky, Drosselmeyer—were plowing through the Triple Crown races, in front of hundreds of thousands of fans and national television audiences, with million-dollar purses on the line, Lisa's Booby Trap was quietly working out in the obscurity of Finger Lakes Racetrack, in the gloom and mud of an upstate spring.

With each passing day she grew stronger and more confident, her stride smoother, longer, less labored. There was something else Tim noticed (and Tebbutt noticed it, as well): the filly's temperament improved dramatically. Those reluctant to seek mystical reasons for the behavior of animals might point to the fact that just about any creature—including human beings—is prone to orneriness when it doesn't feel well. Chronic pain will wear away at the spirit of even the strongest animal. If it's true that Tim Snyder had alleviated a substantial portion of Lisa's discomfort by correcting her feet and shoulder problems, then it makes sense that she would have developed into a less irritable animal around the barn. Popular mythology notwithstanding, a gentle demeanor is hardly a prerequisite for success among thoroughbred racehorses. Ask anyone who has spent a reasonable amount of time in the sport, and you'll hear stories of champions who routinely tried to sever the digits of anyone foolish enough to hand-feed them in the stall; or bucked so hard in the paddock that they unseated their riders. Whatever strand of DNA it is that makes a horse fiercely competitive when the starting gate is thrown open can also make him pure hell to be around.

Conversely, a horse who likes to nuzzle its handlers in the barn might lack the fire to run. Or not. This much is certain: Lisa's Booby Trap, who had been frequently glum and reluctant, and sometimes downright nasty, when Tim Snyder first took possession of her, became a more compliant and personable filly on the backstretch of Finger Lakes Racetrack. It was almost as if someone had slipped Prozac into her feedbag. With this sweeter disposition came an improved work ethic at the track. The changes were at first subtle—a livelier gait, less tenderness after walking or breezing—and then more glaring. All of this happened anecdotally, and out of the field of vision of anyone who might care, for Lisa's improvement was measured only by instinct. A horse can exhibit the characteristics of a runner, but until you put a clock on her it's all just wishful thinking.

Tim was hesitant in those first few weeks to formally test his filly. Nevertheless, it had become apparent to both Snyder and Tebbutt that Lisa was looking less like her stablemates at Finger Lakes, and more like a horse who belonged at Belmont or Saratoga. Her improvement went largely unnoticed, but at any racetrack there are people looking for the long shot who isn't really a long shot; a horse who will go off at healthy odds, despite the fact that she's actually quite capable of winning. The same mind-set applies to would-be owners and trainers, virtually all of whom spend a good deal of their time angling for new product.

"One guy around the barn watched her work a few times," Tim remembered, "and I could tell he was impressed. He kept saying, 'When are you gonna run that filly? I like the way she looks.'"

"Couple weeks, maybe," Tim told him.

"Yeah? Maiden special weights?"

"Could be," Tim said coyly.

The other man smiled. "Well, if she runs one, two, or three, I'll give you twenty-five grand for her."

At first, Tim said nothing, simply nodded and clenched his jaw to keep from shouting at the sky.

Twenty-five grand?! Just for hitting the board?

He'd been around long enough to know that horse racing is a poker game, with bluffs and bullshit an integral part of the process. Maybe the man was serious; maybe not. Regardless, the unwritten rules of the sport dictated that Snyder feign disinterest. Like a football player reaching the end zone for the first time, he had two choices: dance like a celebratory fool, and risk being branded a novice . . . or act like he'd been there before.

Tim chose the latter option.

With a hand resting on Lisa's forehead, he looked at the man and offered a true horse trader's salvo.

"Who said she's for sale?"

The man laughed. "They're all for sale, Timmy."

Of course she was. They both knew it. Right?

At backstretches across the country, at tracks large and small, prosperous and failing; from Churchill Downs to the county fair circuit, horse racing is driven by two things: the gambler's dollar and the horseman's passion. But even a soft-hearted trainer knows better than to allow himself to grow too attached to his stock. Horses are raised and developed and trained with a single goal in mind: to turn a profit for their owners. That doesn't mean they don't sometimes provoke tender responses in the people who work with them on a daily basis; it simply means that everyone in the game understands the parameters, and a certain hardness will probably make success more likely, and failure a bit more tolerable.

Lisa Calley was a *horse lover* first, a *horseman* second.

Tim Snyder was a horseman first, second, third, and beyond.

"You know, I'll sell you anything," he would say later that summer, while standing improbably, almost shockingly, outside a barn at venerable Saratoga Race Course. "Ask anyone who knows me. I'll sell you my truck, the clothes off my back. I've sold just about every horse I've ever owned. Never got attached to any of them."

Until Lisa's Booby Trap came along.

"This is horse is different," he said, shaking his head in disbelief. "This is personal. I'll never sell her."

In April, though, Tim wasn't so sure, and most proclamations about the big bay filly not being on the market were merely misdirection. And yet . . . there was something about her that gave him pause. Maybe it was simply a matter of stature. Lisa was one hell of a handsome horse, as physically impressive as any animal Snyder had ever owned. When he took her by the reins and led her from the barn to the track, he could feel the strength in his hands. When he entered her stall, he couldn't help but be impressed by the sheer size of the filly.

Consider for a moment that Zenyatta, arguably the greatest filly in history, stood 17.2 hands high, and was considered an absolute beast—physiologically on par with the top male horses of her generation. Secretariat, known colloquially as "Big Red," stood 16.2 hands high. At 17.5 hands, Lisa was taller than either of those horses, taller in fact than just about any horse. Of course, there's more to the making of a racehorse than simply height. But Lisa was strong as well, her body gaining muscle mass and tone with each passing week. If you were a racetrack lifer, wheeling and dealing crappy, slow-footed stock, buying one day, selling the next, never seeing anything pass through your barn that could remotely be mistaken for a Grade I–caliber racehorse, let alone a Triple Crown contender, and suddenly you found yourself bathing a filly seventeen hands tall, with the rippling musculature of a true runner . . . well, you could be forgiven for losing your shit; maybe even for falling in love.

"Right from the beginning, Timmy was very attached to this horse," observed Carol Calley. "It wasn't like him to be that way. And I know it sounds funny, but the horse was very attached to him, too."

The romantic might suggest that the trainer saw something in the horse, beyond merely her name, that reminded him of his late wife. Certainly, as time passed, Tim did nothing to dissuade that notion. If others wanted to weave a sentimental story, well, that was their business. If sportswriters and bloggers felt compelled to grasp at the obvious, fantastic hook—that Lisa Calley had made good on her deathbed promise of returning to life as a racehorse—there was no reason to argue otherwise.

"I don't know about all that reincarnation stuff," Tim would say at the height of the frenzy. "I mean, she's a horse. But I will say this: I talk with her all the time. I tell her about my day. I tell her how I'm doing. And I do it just like I used to talk with my old lady."

He stopped, smiled sheepishly.

"I know how that sounds: kind of crazy. But that's what I do."

There are so many possible explanations for Snyder's initial interest in the horse, and for his reluctance to give her up in those first few months. Yes, she was strikingly attractive, but as she gained confidence and fitness, she offered more than merely aesthetic pleasures. Ego and ambition (and maybe a bit of greed) are powerful motivators in any business, and the horseman is hardly invulnerable to these factors. Tim Snyder had never owned or trained a great racehorse; hell, he'd only owned or trained a handful of even competent racehorses. He'd spent his whole life around horses—breaking, training, grooming and shipping them; buying them and selling them with virtually no emotional investment or any hope of hitting the jackpot—and now, all of a sudden, he had a horse in his barn (well, in John Tebbutt's barn) that might just be something special. A horse that looked and behaved like a real racehorse. A horse no one else wanted or believed in. He had found her and fixed her, and he rightfully took no small amount of pride in that accomplishment.

Indisputably, racing is a cruel and fickle game, thus the prevailing wisdom is this: If you're lucky enough to have a good horse, cash in as quickly as possible. You're never more than one bad step away from a crippling injury (and, subsequently, a lethal injection); one bad performance away from being worthless on the breeding market.

No one had to tell any of this to Tim Snyder. He knew better than anyone that logic and common sense dictated that if someone wanted to buy his $4,500 filly for twenty-five grand, he should get down on his knees, thank God for his unexpected good fortune, take the money, pay off his debts, fix his Taurus wagon, maybe get some decent health insurance, and find a place of his own to live. Then, and only then, if there were a few bucks left over, maybe he could buy another horse. You take whatever victories you find in this game, and you measure success in the smallest of increments.

Tim Snyder considered all of this carefully. But as the mud of April dried and the winter winds blowing off Canandaigua Lake relented—a sure sign that racing season was on the horizon—Tim began to have second thoughts. For the first time in a long time, he listened to his heart rather than his head.

Maybe I'll hang on to her for a while.

Chapter Eleven

Horse racing is not so much a business as it is a calling. The work requires too much time and energy to pursue it with anything less than utter passion; and even then, the odds against success can seem practically insurmountable. But for those who are drawn into the game, particularly at a young age, success and failure are almost irrelevant. Theirs is an obsession that must be fed, often without regard to the usual societal constraints, or the expectations set forth by family and friends.

They are at home only on the backstretch. They are at peace—to the extent that they can find peace—only on the back of a horse.

Tim Snyder was like that. To a slightly lesser extent, so was Janice Blake-Baeza.

She had arrived at Finger Lakes Racetrack in April 2010,

with a long but hardly overwhelming resume as a jockey, and virtually no contacts. She could hear the clock ticking, too. Horse racing is more forgiving of the passing years than many sports—it's not uncommon to see a forty-something rider among the leaders in the jockey standings—but as in any athletic endeavor, youth is generally coveted. At nearly forty-five years of age, Blake-Baeza was inching toward the twilight of her competitive career, and the shadows, quite frankly, scared the shit out of her. She'd been at Philadelphia Park all winter, watching and waiting, trying unsuccessfully to drum up work, and so she came to Upstate New York with the hope of gaining some traction in a career that had mainly been about slipping and sliding.

"I've always enjoyed New York, and I wanted to be at Belmont and Aqueduct in the fall and winter, so I thought I'd start out by going to Finger Lakes for the summer," Blake-Baeza said. "But I didn't know anybody there, really. I knew faces, but I didn't have a barn behind me; no one who was going to put me on horses. I just drove up there cold and said, 'Here I am.'"

Blake-Baeza's story is quixotic in the way of so many racetrack biographies. She grew up around horses, took part in dressage and steeplechase competitions, then mostly put it aside in favor of more traditional pursuits, like college and career. With a biology degree in hand she went to work in a hospital lab, but the tug of the racetrack would not subside. In the late 1990s she traded a white coat for colorful silks and began chasing her dream: to become a world-class jockey.

She'd been a working rider for a dozen years by the time she got to Finger Lakes, with more than 2,500 starts and many thousands of hours logged as an exercise rider all over the East Coast. But the breakthrough had never come. Blake-Baeza's career winning percentage (meaning the number of times her horses had finished in the money—first, second, or third) hovered around 25 percent, a dismal figure when compared with the game's top riders, who typically will be closer to 50 percent in any given meet. Much of this was beyond Blake-Baeza's control. You can't win on a slow horse; paradoxically, you can't get trainers to put you on fast horses unless you've proven you can win (usually on the slower horses).

This was the nearly universal jockey's conundrum, and Blake-Baeza had been dealing with it for years. If there was a twist to her story, it could be found in her last name: she was married to Braulio Baeza, a retired Hall of Fame jockey. Whether Blake-Baeza was helped by that connection or hindered by the skepticism and sexism (and the burden of unrealistic expectation) that naturally came with it is difficult to say. But one thing is certain: When she came to Finger Lakes, Blake-Baeza needed work, and she wasn't the least bit fussy about where she was going to find it.

Her search began at the barn of John Tebbutt.

"Someone had told me to see him, because he's willing to ride girls," Blake-Baeza remembered. "He told me he could pay me for exercise work, so I said fine, thinking maybe he'd use me as a jockey, too."

Tebbutt was noncommittal on that point, but Blake-Baeza quickly found herself chatting with another trainer in Tebbutt's barn; a trainer with only one horse, but what an attractive horse she was. The trainer's name was Tim Snyder. The horse was Lisa's Booby Trap.

"Tim was kind of breaking down physically at that time," Blake-Baeza said. "He really couldn't get on the horse every day. He knew I needed the money, and that I was looking for work, so he asked me to ride Lisa in the mornings. I had no history with him, but I could tell he knew the game. I mean, he's a talker, too. Second day I was there, I knew the whole story: how he slept in his car, lived in a tack room at the track with feces on the wall; I knew the horse had a clubfoot and she was blind in one eye, and this and that. Whatever. It was Finger Lakes, not Belmont; you roll with it. Tim was a good horseman. If you've been around a while, you can tell if it's real or smoke and mirrors, and I could tell with Tim that he knew what he was doing. He's the real deal.

"Lisa didn't run well in the beginning because she was hurting, and it's hard to run when you're in pain," Blake-Baeza went on. "Tim understood that. He's a very intuitive horseman. He knows horses like that guy [Tom Smith] who trained Seabiscuit. He can feel the horse, know what's going on just by rubbing his hands over her. Tim is quirky, yes, but that's what happens when you're that in tune with another creature, another being: you lose other parts of your life."

Like so many racetrack arrangements, this one was done on a handshake: Blake-Baeza would work the filly in the morning, get to know her personality, help her grow accustomed to the rigors of the starting gate. If everything worked out as planned, they'd be listed together as jockey and horse when Lisa's Booby Trap made her first start.

"That happens all the time at the racetrack," Blake-Baeza said. "You work the horse and you build a relationship with the trainer. Then you ride the horse. Usually, though, it's not a horse like Lisa. It's a five-thousand-dollar claimer, at best. First time I got on her, I just knew: This was like providence. It was God's will, directing me, saying, 'This horse is for you.'"

It was after one spirited morning workout—just an informal breeze along the backside, with hardly anyone watching—that Blake-Baeza confirmed to Tim and John Tebbutt what they both had suspected: "I think you've got a stake horse here."

Anecdotal information is not to be dismissed, especially when offered by someone who has been around the track a time or two. Still, talk is cheap. In the horse racing world, numbers are everything; a $4,500 filly is simply that until she proves otherwise, and there is documented evidence to support the transformation.

In the case of Lisa's Booby Trap, the ascent out of obscurity began on April 17, 2010. This was the filly's first official workout. Rather than just breezing, her effort would be recorded by one of the track's clockers, with the results posted in the *Daily Racing Form,* the bible of the racing industry and the primary tool for handicappers and anyone else who follows the sport. If it turned out she could really run—if, say, she turned in the fastest workout of the day, known as a "bullet" in racing parlance—then everyone would know it; if she turned out to be a dog, well, they'd know that, too.

Published workout times take on an air of importance that is not always warranted. For one thing, it's not necessarily true that a horse is being driven to the full extent of its capabilities in a workout; only the horse's handlers know how hard she was running, and whether the workout demanded more of her than anticipated. Complicating matters further is the possibility, however remote, that the published time is simply not accurate; that for any number of reasons, ranging from human or technological error to deliberate manipulation, the horse's workout time has been in some way altered.

"Oh, that's not just Finger Lakes, that's everywhere," Blake-Baeza said. "Some owners want to see the bullet every time. Others don't; they just want the horse to work. Let's say you work three furlongs, and the horse goes thirty-four (seconds). The trainer might call up the clocker and say, 'Please don't put down thirty-four. Just put thirty-six in the paper.' Stuff like that happens every day—*every single day*—at racetracks all over the country. It's part of the game."

To illustrate her point, Blake-Baeza told the story of a prominent racehorse, a colt talented enough to win a Triple Crown event in the early 2000s. One day at Aqueduct Racetrack, shortly after the colt had turned three years old (and well before he had emerged as a potential champion), Blake-Baeza found herself alongside him in the starting gate, on a different mount.

"He got left in the gate, literally ten lengths behind the field at the first call," she remembered. "I'm in front at the eighth pole, winning the race, when suddenly this blur goes by me. I finish second, lose to this horse. Then I go back to the *Racing Form*, and look at the workouts: all 50s, and 49s (for four furlongs). And this horse is like 10-1? And he goes on to win (a Triple Crown race)? There's just no way."

The first official, timed workout for Lisa's Booby Trap came at a distance of four furlongs, on an early spring day at Finger Lakes. Her time, over a track surface classified as "good," was a respectable 50.6 seconds, in a workout that Snyder described as "not that hard." Two and a half weeks later, on May 4, Lisa returned to the track for her second official workout, this time on an uncommonly bright, clear day, over a track labeled "fast."

Unlike most races (steeplechase events being the exception), workouts sometimes begin informally, with the rider galloping the horse back and forth, until eventually reaching the "starting line," which is nothing more than one of the track's marker poles (which are placed at intervals of one sixteenth of a mile all around the track), a specified distance from the finish line. He'll jog the horse to that point, then urge his mount to begin running hard, while an assortment of clockers—official and unofficial (trainers, owners, handicappers, gamblers)—stand at the ready. On other occasions, though, the horse will work out of a starting gate, which was the case with Lisa's Booby Trap on this day.

"She almost left the jockey in the gate, that's how fast she went out," Snyder recalled with a laugh. "But the horse ducked a little bit, just out of greenness."

Blake-Baeza remembered the trip vividly, particularly the start.

"Maybe because she was blind in that one eye, she came out of the gate and sort of made a hard turn," Blake-Baeza said. "I didn't fall, but I slipped off the side of her, and I was riding her Indian-style all the way across the chute. She went maybe ten strides with me hanging off the side. It was scary.

But I got myself back up there, and she was very professional about it. Didn't stop or bolt or anything."

Once righted, Lisa found her stride and quickly went to the lead among a small group of horses working together.

"She was in there with two other horses," Snyder recalled. "A couple veterans that had made some money, older horses, and after she caught up, she just left them all behind."

While Snyder knew Lisa was running well almost as soon as she found her rhythm, what he saw as she crossed the finish line still surprised him. Her time, according to his watch, was a shade over forty-five seconds, which would have earned a bullet at just about any track in the country on most days.

At Finger Lakes Racetrack it was an anomaly of almost epic proportions.

"She did it easy, too," Snyder recalled. "So graceful. There were a few guys with watches, and we all had her in about the same time, all between forty-five and forty-six. At first I thought maybe I hit the button at the wrong pole—that's how fast she was. You don't get many 45s at Finger Lakes. Forget workouts—you don't even get 45s in the afternoon, when they're racing. The cat was out of the bag then. I knew she'd be a short price after that."

Not as short as she might have been, for the published time on Lisa's four-furlong workout that day was 47.4 seconds, still a solid number, but not quite reflective of the jaw-dropping performance she apparently had turned in. Snyder said he wasn't aware of the discrepancy between his watch and the official watch until later that morning, when times were posted. His reaction: a shrug of the shoulders.

"That happens sometimes, especially at small tracks. But

I know what she ran. And if she hadn't come out of the gate sideways, she might have gone forty-four."

Later that afternoon, Snyder said, one of the track's clockers showed up at Tebbutt's barn, angling for Lisa's Booby Trap.

"He told me it was the fastest time he'd ever seen at Finger Lakes," Snyder said. "And he was interested in buying the horse, or brokering her for another guy. So maybe he wrote the work slower than it was to keep people away. I don't know."

Snyder listened as the man made his pitch.

"I got a guy in Florida who will buy her for forty thousand dollars."

Tim did not hesitate before answering, probably because he knew that if he thought long and hard enough, and allowed logic to enter the equation, he might part ways with his prized filly.

"That's a nice offer," he said. But I'm not selling her."

Some time later, long after the market value of Lisa's Booby Trap had soared and plummeted, Snyder tried to explain his line of thinking.

"I figured, I've gone this far with her, I might as well keep going, see what she can do. By now I've got a connection with her. We've made a lot of progress together."

Snyder paused, waved a hand dismissively.

"I've been around a lot of goddamn money in my day. Worked for a lot of rich people, had some money myself. I've bought cars and trucks and other stuff, and none of it mattered much. None of it makes you happy. It's material shit, and it don't matter. You have it for a while, and then it's gone. This was my horse."

By the time late May rolled around, Janice Blake-Baeza had also developed a personal and proprietary interest in Lisa's Booby Trap. The journeyman rider felt an understandable kinship with the overlooked and underappreciated filly. If the horse had more talent than she had been given credit for, well, then maybe the same was true of her rider. It takes only one great horse to forever alter the career of a trainer or jockey, and maybe, for Blake-Baeza, this was the horse.

Then again, maybe not.

Although a regular around John Tebbutt's barn, and unfailing in her commitment to galloping Lisa's Booby Trap whenever Tim Snyder required her services, Blake-Baeza could hardly make a living on one horse. So, in the time-honored tradition of racetrack hustling, she showed up on the backstretch each morning, chatted up trainers and owners, and slowly developed a clientele. One trainer, in particular, Pat Baratta, thought highly enough of Blake-Baeza to assign her multiple mounts in the morning, the implication being that if any of these horses made it to the starting gate, she would get first call as jockey. Among the most promising of these horses was a four-year-old mare named Sandy Castle.

"A nice horse," Blake-Baeza said, "and I'm working her every morning, same as I'm doing for Tim and Lisa. But Pat is my big stable. He likes me, he's going to give me work."

All well and good until Baratta and his mentor, Danny

Poliziani—who was listed as Sandy Castle's official trainer for a short period in 2010—decided to enter their horse in the sixth race at Finger Lakes, on May 24, a six-furlong allowance race for fillies and mares three years of age and older.

The very same race in which Lisa's Booby Trap would be making her debut.

Janice Blake-Baeza had the call on both girls. She'd come to Finger Lakes without an agent or any guarantee of steady work and suddenly, it seemed, she had more opportunities than she could handle.

"What a fiasco," Blake-Baeza said. "I got Lisa's Booby Trap—one broke-down guy with one horse—and I got this other guy, Pat Baratta, who's got money and a whole barn. Lisa's a good horse, but I'm still not one hundred percent sure she can beat Sandy, who's also a good horse. I'm watching all this develop, and I'm thinking, 'This can't be happening!' I'm lucky to get six rides a week at Finger Lakes, and now I've got a double-call? With two good horses? Unbelievable!"

Divine intervention notwithstanding, Blake-Baeza let practicality and common sense guide her decision. She committed to Sandy Castle, ensuring that that there would be a steady stream of work in the coming weeks and months, but leaving Lisa's Booby Trap without a rider just a few days before her first race. Not that this was unusual in horse racing. Trainers drop jockeys and jockeys drop trainers all the time, for any number of reasons, ranging from conflicting commitments to disputes over job performance.

In this case it was simply a matter of the rider making the prudent choice.

"I have to ride Pat's horse," Blake-Baeza told Snyder one morning on the backstretch.

Tim accepted the news reluctantly.

"It's your decision," he said, "but I think you're making a mistake. This is a nice horse."

"I know," the jockey said. "I'm sorry."

Those who have been around Tim Snyder for any length of time, and have seen how openly he wears his heart on his sleeve, might be surprised to learn that he expressed not a trace of anger.

"Tim was cool about it," Blake-Baeza noted. "He knows the racetrack and he knows what you've gotta do to survive. It's not like I didn't know it might happen; we had talked about the possibility. I had a choice, but it wasn't a very good choice. What would happen if I took off Pat's barn and rode Lisa, and she finishes up the track? And the jockey on Pat's horse wins the race? First of all I look like an idiot, and now I'm not in Pat's barn anymore. I couldn't ride both horses, so I had to pick one. Believe me, I didn't want to do it. I even asked Pat to scratch his horse and enter her the next week."

Snyder did not have to look far for a replacement rider, and once again he selected a female jockey for his filly. Her name was Elaine Castillo, and she had long been a favorite of John Tebbutt's.

"Nothing against the other rider, but I was delighted when Timmy picked up Elaine," Tebbutt said. "She was another one of those really nice people you come across sometimes. Just a sweetheart of a person, and she got along great with horses; she had a natural way with them."

Like most people on the Finger Lakes backstretch, Castillo by this point had heard about the one-eyed, clubfooted filly. In fact, she'd first gotten word of the filly a few months earlier, when she was galloping horses and racing for Tebbutt in Florida. Tim Snyder would occasionally run his mouth about this new horse he'd acquired, and how she was enormously talented and could one day make a hell of a racehorse—if he could only get her straightened out.

"I've known Tim for quite a while, actually," Castillo said with a laugh. "He's a bullshitter, so when Timmy talks . . . well, you believe what you want to believe. I'd never worked for him, but I knew some people who don't like him—a few riders who said you couldn't trust him, that he'd promise you a ride and then sting you at the last second. But I try to get along with everyone, and Timmy was a friend of John's, so we were fine. In Florida he kept telling me about this horse, and how no one else could even breeze her, she was so messed up, but he was going to turn her around. I just listened and thought, *Okay, Timmy, have fun with that.*"

By late May Castillo knew the filly was in Tebbutt's barn, supposedly training well, and that Snyder had burdened her with some ridiculous name. ("Only Timmy would do something like that.") In all candor, that's about all she wanted to know—until she was approached by Tebbutt just a few days before the filly was to race for the first time.

"She's available," Tebbut said. "I think you should ride her. She's going to do great."

Had it been anyone else, Castillo would have declined the offer.

"But John was my guy," she said. "And the filly was under his name. If not for John, who I trust and who wants the best for me, I wouldn't have considered her."

Whatever skepticism Castillo harbored, it melted away the next morning, when she climbed aboard Lisa for an introductory gallop.

"Wow, she looked good," Castillo recalled. "She was this big, huge filly, and she moved so well. At that point I immediately started to feel pressure. I mean, she was a first-time starter, and sometimes people are worried they might be bad or misbehave. I thought maybe that's what had happened with Janice taking off. But if she'd been working her the whole time, she should have known how good [Lisa] might be. It didn't really matter; that stuff happens on the track all the time. I was just grateful for the opportunity."

On May 24, the sixth race at Finger Lakes was an allowance race with a purse of twenty thousand dollars. At Belmont or Saratoga, that would be a decidedly minor event; at Finger Lakes it was the feature race of the day. As he would do virtually every time she ran, Tim Snyder spent much of the day with Lisa's Booby Trap, hanging out by her stall, chatting with her—or at her, as the case may be—ostensibly trying to keep her calm, but really just trying to maintain control of his own frayed nerves.

Shortly before three o'clock he led the filly out of her stall and began the long walk to the paddock area. Horses, most trainers will tell you, thrive on routine; they can also be shaken by routine. A horse racing for the very first time does not know what to expect, and thus her handlers have no way of knowing what to expect from her. Once seasoned, a horse is likely to be highly spirited, even to the point of agitation, as she goes through the race-day routine, for she knows that inevitably she will end up in a starting gate, crammed alongside ten other anxious horses, and that soon she'll be running so hard that she might bleed from her nostrils. She associates prerace prep with pain and discomfort.

For even the most naturally competitive and gifted of horses, race day is one filled with anxiety and unpredictable behavior.

To Lisa's Booby Trap, all this pampering and parading was new. She had no frame of reference, and so she reacted indifferently. As she walked from her barn to the track, with Tim holding the reins, she seemed completely relaxed—until they reached the entrance of the track, near the quarter-pole chute, and found themselves temporarily blocked by one of the track's maintenance trucks as it went about the business of watering down the track. (This is ordinary maintenance that occurs between races, to keep the surface from drying out). As the truck passed, then stopped, Tim led his filly onto the track.

"That's when I almost lost her," he recalled. "The truck had stopped, then the guy opened his door and jumped out, and the noise spooked Lisa. She ran backwards, and I went with her. Then I couldn't get her past the water truck, because she was so nervous. It took me a while to get her settled down."

By the time Lisa arrived in the paddock, she had been made a 6-5 favorite by the betting crowd at Finger Lakes, who no doubt were swayed by the filly's strong workout record, as well as the fact that, as a newcomer, she would be carrying only 118 pounds, six pounds less than Sandy Castle. None of this mattered much to John Tebbutt, who paced nervously in anticipation of the filly's arrival.

"Where have you been?" he asked Snyder. "You're going to get me fined for being late."

Tim scoffed.

"Let 'em fine me. I don't give a damn, as long as they fine the guy driving the water truck, too."

At 3:24 P.M., Lisa's Booby Trap broke cleanly, if not enthusiastically, from the seven hole—the far outside in a seven-horse field—and rushed quickly to the front alongside a 31-1 long shot named She's An Outlaw. They hit the quarter-mile mark together in a swift 22.58 seconds; by the half-mile mark, passed in 46.1, She's An Outlaw was laboring, and Lisa had begun to pull away.

"She broke well and she ran easy . . . I mean *easy*," Castillo said. "None of us really knew how much horse there would be, but she was strong and steady. Obviously she impressed everyone."

Indeed she did, including racetrack announcer Tony Calo, who marveled at the filly as she romped through the stretch, essentially under a hand ride from Castillo (meaning the jockey rarely used her whip), while pulling away to a 17 ¾-length victory. She covered the six furlongs, or three-quarters of a mile, over a track labeled "fast," in 1:10.40, an inaugural performance so lopsided that it would have raised eyebrows at virtually any track in the country.

"Check out this debut-er!" Calo shouted. "Lisa's Booby Trap, *very* impressive in her first look. She is an authoritative winner! And it's a good running time."

Then, after an uncomfortably long pause (or maybe not, given the gap between the two horses), Calo resumed calling the race.

"Sandy Castle for second . . ."

At a handful of elegant, genteel racetracks—Saratoga, Del Mar, Churchill Downs—where great flocks of tourists not only help fuel the business but also diminish the harshness of the clientele, a rider often spends much of his time on the long walk back to the jockeys' room signing autographs and shaking hands with fans. This is not the case at most tracks, where virtually every attendee is either a hard-core racing fan or a degenerate gambler. Either way, they hate to lose, and given the rather obvious fact that horses don't give a damn how much money you bet on them, racetrack patrons must look elsewhere to heave their scorn.

As often as not, it's the rider who shoulders the blame.

And so, as she walked from the track to the jocks' quarters after the race, Janice Blake-Baeza tried to ignore the taunting and the sarcasm hurled her way by a small but vocal Finger Lakes crowd.

"Smart move, girl!"

"That could have been you on that horse!"

Walking briskly, eyes straight ahead, Blake-Baeza said nothing in response. They had paid their money; they could say whatever they wanted. She had been around far too long to take any of it personally. As much as she loved the sport, she hated the hardness that it provoked in some people. The meanness. Like so many other things, though, it was part of the game.

"What are you gonna do?" she would later say. "It's not the *Jerry Springer Show*. You can't yell back at them. You make your decision and live with it. You move on. You don't chew your arm off over it."

Chapter Twelve

Shortly before six o'clock on the morning of May 25, John Shaw's phone began ringing. Predawn calls are not unusual in the world of horse racing, where the workday typically begins under the cover of darkness, so Shaw felt no urgency to pick up the line. Instead, he went about his business and let the call kick over to voice mail. A few minutes later, he checked the message.

It was from George Burrows, the trainer at Ocala Stud who had served as a conduit between Shaw and Michael O'Farrell in the exchange of a tall, unnamed, slow-footed horse nearly one year earlier.

"Hey, you hear about that filly we sent to you? She won by seventeen and a half lengths yesterday at Finger Lakes!"

It was a short message, and it failed to communicate

perhaps the most important piece of information: the horse's name. So Shaw quickly returned the call.

"What filly are you talking about?" he asked.

"The Drewman filly," Burrows replied, offering up not the name of the horse, but rather its sire.

The line went quiet for a moment as Shaw racked his brain for some hint of recognition. He'd moved a lot of horses over the years, and more than a few had come to him from Ocala Stud. Finally, it dawned on him.

"Not the Drewman filly *I* had?" he said, his voice echoing nothing so much as bewilderment.

"Yup, that's the one," Burrows said. "Can you believe it?"

Frankly, no, Shaw could not believe it. Free horses became barn ponies; they did not win races by seventeen and a half lengths, not even at Finger Lakes. And even by the ridiculously low standards of horses deemed unworthy of sale, this filly had been disappointing. Attractive, yes, but just about the slowest filly God had ever put on Earth; slowest one Shaw had ever seen, anyway. That this filly had somehow evolved into a running machine stretched the limits of incredulity.

"Can't be the same horse," he said. "Somebody better go up there and check, because it has to be a ringer."

Burrows assured him that it was, in fact, the very same filly—the one Shaw had acquired without a request for compensation, and that he had passed on to fellow broker Don Hunt, who in turn had sold the horse to a guy in Upstate New York for $4,500, only a portion of which had made its way to Shaw. Not only had she won, but she had done so in her very first race, and in a time that would make her breeders proud to acknowledge her pedigree: 1:10 and change for six furlongs.

Shaw stared off into space and said nothing.

The Drewman filly . . . Well, I'll be damned.

Equally amused, but hardly disappointed, was Michael O'Farrell, the manager of Ocala Stud.

"When she won her first start, we were all surprised," he said. "It wasn't just that she won the race, but that she ran such a fast time and won so convincingly. And, of course, we called and kidded with John Shaw. He didn't mind, I don't think. We've all been in the business a long time. There's nothing you can be upset about. It's just one of those things that no one could have predicted. It's a shocker, but it's good, too. A story like this is good for the sport. It attracts fans. And it's certainly not bad for us. Anytime a horse from our farm runs well, it's good for business. So there were no regrets about letting her go. We were pleased. I mean, it wasn't like she was going to make or break our year, but you're always happy to see the horses you raised or sold go out and do well; at the end of the day it shows up as another horse from Ocala Stud that's been successful. That's a good thing."

Horse racing is an insular world, its denizens competing in an increasingly overlooked sport; so, impressive as it was, the inaugural performance of Lisa's Booby Trap remained something of an arcane achievement—at least for a little while. Yes, traffic increased somewhat around John Tebbutt's barn, as did the price offered for Lisa's Bobby Trap, from twenty-five thousand to forty thousand. Tim Snyder didn't so much as blink. By this point he had grown extraordinarily close to the horse, spending virtually every waking hour at her stall and sleeping just a short distance away, in a tack room at Finger Lakes. She represented to him so many things that he had lost or forgotten, or never possessed in the first place: opportunity, hope, pride, and, yes, love. She was the culmination of a life's work, a totem of his late wife and a potential winning lottery ticket, all rolled into one. She gave him purpose; she got him out of bed in the morning.

Would he trade all of that for forty grand? Not a chance.

But the numbers were about to mushroom, and with the expansion came temptation—and pressure—that Snyder had never anticipated.

On June 12 Lisa's Booby Trap returned to Finger Lakes for the second start of her career, in a $19,000 allowance race for fillies and mares. There would be no surprises this time, no sneaking up on the competition or the betting populace. Lisa was assigned 119 pounds, second highest weight in the field; nevertheless, she was a heavy morning-line favorite, and by race time she was an almost comically prohibitive 1-9 choice in a six-horse field.

As in her debut, Lisa would be competing over six furlongs on a dry, fast, dirt track. In the saddle, for the second consecutive time, was Elaine Castillo. Watching from the sidelines was Janice Blake-Baeza, who would never again ride Lisa's Booby Trap.

"It was Elaine's horse pretty much after that first race," Blake-Baeza said, the disappointment palpable in her voice. "She was in with John Tebbutt, and John was a friend of her agent, and obviously the agent wasn't going to let that one get away, not after the way she ran. So they all had a history together. Tim owed John Tebbutt, big-time, and John wanted his rider on that horse in the first place. He always wanted Elaine, so who knows what went on behind the scene. But once she got on the horse, they weren't about to make a change. I tried talking to Tim. 'I've put in all this work; I think you should give me the ride back second race.' But he said, 'Nope, can't do that. I'm sorry.' I think that was John's decision more than Tim's, but what are you going to do? Elaine's a good rider and she was in the right place at the right time."

A footnote worth mentioning is that while Blake-Baeza was not happy with losing the mount, she appreciated the fact that a couple months later, as the career earnings of Lisa continued to swell, Tim Snyder recognized the rider's contribution.

"He did stake me," Blake-Baeza said. "He gave me some money, which was nice of him."

Drawing an inside position, Lisa broke well for the second straight time and went directly to the lead. She ran comfortably through the half-mile mark, setting a brisk but manageable pace and keeping the completion on her shoulder, a length or two behind, until she round the final turn and began her stretch run. The moment Castillo showed her whip and exhorted the big filly to move, she did so with ease, efficiently opening up a lead of five lengths by the eighth pole. As Castillo dug into the horse for the stretch run, Lisa took on the appearance of a horse that had stumbled into the wrong race; indeed, she looked again like the ringer that John Shaw had mentioned.

The winning margin was ten and a half lengths, the winning time 1:10.38, almost identical to her first race. A bet on Lisa's Booby Trap returned a modest $2.20 for a two-dollar investment. For her handlers, though, she earned more than eleven thousand dollars, bringing her career winnings to more than twenty thousand. Not exactly the stuff of legend, but not bad for a $4,500 Finger Lakes filly.

"You know, there were times with Lisa where she'd be a little sore during workouts," Castillo recalled. "Her ankle would get swollen, and sometimes you'd see her walking by, kind of favoring it. But then she'd get out and race, and . . . oh, my goodness, what a heart! As long as she was even a little bit okay, that girl could run. Every single time I rode her in a race she was awesome. And I didn't even have to ask her for much. At some point before the second race, Tim had said to me, 'Let's see what she's got. Even if you're at the front, open her up a little bit.' So I did, and you could tell right away she was that good, which was pretty neat."

Neat . . .

Such a quaint and unassuming description, and one that accurately reflects the difference and distance between those who are in horse racing primarily because they love horses and crave competition—jockeys, for example—and those who view it primarily as a business venture. Horses, after all, are commodities, and like any commodity they can at times provoke irrational exuberance on the part of investors. In greener times, when tax codes were friendlier and the sport of thoroughbred racing more popular and self-sustaining, yearling sales would routinely produce stupefying transactions. At the highest levels, horse sales (auctions, by any other name) have always been driven more by vanity and greed than common sense or wisdom. The yearling sale is all about *potential*—the possibility that a gangly colt might someday win the Kentucky Derby and bring his new owners fame and fortune. (Okay, the fortune part they likely already have, but a winning horse is at least worth bragging rights at the polo club or the marina.) Millions of dollars are tossed at horses that have never run a competitive step, and might never see the inside of a starting gate.

But that's the precisely the point. In many cases a horse with stout lineage is never worth more on the open market than he is at a yearling sale, when the entire breadth and depth of his résumé consists of a single line: the one denoting his parents. If he turns out to be a runner in his own right, his value goes up; if not, his value plummets, dragging the value of future generations in its wake. This is why it's not uncommon for a horse to be retired shortly after it wins its biggest race, even though it is in perfectly good health. Once a horse wins a Triple Crown race, or a Breeders Cup event, its value as a stud or broodmare skyrockets, and any subsequent trip to the racetrack represents an epic roll of the dice; one or two bad races and the horse is dubbed a fraud, or a freak, or simply lucky, and its stock can fall through the floor.

For a while there, buying a yearling was like buying a tech stock at the height of the Nasdaq boom. It didn't matter that the investment had no proven track record, or any guarantee of returning a dividend, it was simply the *possibility* of greatness—of getting in on the ground floor—that made otherwise reasonable folks swoon.

Lisa's Booby Trap fell into a different category—she possessed neither the stellar racing record of a champion nor the shimmering promise of a yearling born of impeccable breeding. But as a lightly-raced three-year-old with a pair of impressive victories to her credit, she had about her not only the tease of talent, but also the faint whiff of mystery.

Twice she had been to the starting gate, and twice she had won. Twice she had run in a manner befitting a horse that had no business at Finger Lakes. If racing fans had begun to fall in love with the story of the one-eyed wonder horse and the Runyonesque character who found her and nurtured her and somehow brought out the best in her . . . well, others had a more avaristic interest in the filly. And as anyone who has been around the game long enough can tell you, greed wears blinders.

"There's no logic to it," John Tebbutt said with a laugh. "People in this sport spend an awful lot of money on bad horses. And Lisa was a very good horse."

More than that, it seemed—at least to some eyes—for the offers that rained down on Tim Snyder in the aftermath of Lisa's second race were almost enough to shake the owner's loyalty. Fifteen thousand had become forty, forty quickly became fifty, and then one hundred. Now, suddenly, here was Tebbutt, acting as agent, friend, and broker—but mainly just shielding Tim from the pressure and distractions that come with owning a popular racehorse—fielding calls from people with even deeper pockets.

"You take care of it," said Tim, a walking, talking anachronism who had only recently acquired his first cell phone; who had no laptop or Internet connection, and not the slightest idea how to send or a receive a text message. Not so much a technophobe as simply a single-minded man who saw no reason for such devices in his life—and until recently he hadn't the means to acquire them anyway—Snyder leaned on his old buddy and sometime employer for support and guidance. Tebbutt, who was temperamentally better suited for the role anyway, willingly shouldered the responsibility.

"Timmy just couldn't deal with it," Tebbutt recalled. "It was too much for him. Just talking about it got him all flustered and nervous. His solution was to not talk with anyone."

Given that some of the offers came from halfway across the country, while others came from halfway across the track, this made Tebbutt's job challenging, to say the least. The most alluring of the homegrown bids came from Chris Englehart, a longtime trainer and owner whose upstate roots ran deep (he'd grown up in nearby Canandaigua). As a fellow resident of the Finger Lakes backstretch, Englehart had watched Lisa's Booby Trap almost from the day she arrived, and he'd grown sufficiently impressed to offer Snyder (through Tebbutt) as much as $150,000 for the filly.

"Not for sale," Tim declared.

Tebbutt's phone began ringing incessantly, as great chunks of time were devoted to parsing out the legitimacy of the suitors who had somehow gotten his number. Most were easily dissuaded, leading Tebbutt to wonder about their seriousness. It took no great effort, after all, to make a phone call and throw out a few numbers. Tebbutt had been around long enough, and bought and sold enough horses, to distinguish between buyer and bullshitter.

One person whose persistence seemed to place him in the former camp was a bloodstock agent from Kentucky. Tebbutt never met the agent in person but he called repeatedly, claiming to represent a serious buyer from the Midwest. The first offer, Tebbutt said, was $100,000. The second offer, tendered shortly after Lisa's second victory, was $250,000. Each time, Tebbutt took the offer to Tim and each time he declined, but not before consulting with those closest to him. He wondered sometimes whether he was crazy, passing up a quarter million dollars for a horse that had cost only a fraction of that amount.

He called his sister, Cheryl Hall.

"Don't do it," she said. "There's something going on here."

"I just want to do what Lisa would want me to do," Tim said.

This was risky territory, but Cheryl, who knew them both and had come to understand what the filly meant to Tim, took the plunge.

"I think Lisa would want you to keep the horse."

Tim laughed. "I knew you were going to say that!"

In retrospect, it's easy to suggest that Snyder should have unloaded the filly when he had a chance. Interestingly, though, neither Tim nor anyone else close to him expresses any regret about the fact that he may have held onto this particular stock long after it reached a peak.

"The money really didn't matter," said Tebbutt. "Timmy would have found a way to blow all the money anyway. It was the horse that mattered."

Added Tim's sister: "To some extent, we all have a hardened faith in the Lord. My personal belief is that He does things for you. He doesn't put your wife inside a horse; I don't believe that. But I do believe He might send you a horse when you need it most."

Those less susceptible to romanticism dismissed Tim's

loyalty to the filly as the product of either arrogance or stubbornness, if not stupidity.

"I've been training horses for nearly forty years," said Don Hunt. "I don't get surprised by much anymore. But what this horse did surprised me. I was happy for Tim. But you have to understand—to people like Tim, it is not about the money. It's about the love of the horse, and being recognized for having a good horse."

It was pointed out to Hunt that many owners and trainers avoid getting overly connected to their stock for precisely this reason: emotion complicates things; hubris gets in the way of business.

"That's exactly right," Hunt said. "Those guys don't drive three-hundred-dollar station wagons, either."

Occasional sore ankle notwithstanding, Lisa had come out of each of her first two races in good shape, prompting Snyder to reason, logically enough, that the filly seemed to benefit from steady work. So he entered her in a $17,000 allowance race on June 29; the level of competition would be similar to what she had faced previously; this time, though, she would be stretching out to a distance of one mile and 70 yards, a natural progression for a horse relatively new to competition. This would help Snyder determine whether Lisa was a natural sprinter, or more of a middle-distance runner.

Or, perhaps, a bit of both.

Snyder tried to focus on his work, but background noise persisted in the form of an escalation in the bidding war for Lisa's Booby Trap. On the afternoon of June 29, as Tim prepped Lisa in her stall, John Tebbutt's cell phone rang again. Busily helping Tim with prerace matters, Tebbutt let the call kick over to voice mail. A short time later Tebbutt checked his messages. It was the same bloodstock agent, calling to let Tebbutt know that his client would not be easily discouraged, and in fact was prepared to sweeten the deal considerably. At the time, he said, they were at Keeneland Racetrack, preparing to watch the simulcast from Finger Lakes.

"When you see Tim," the bloodstock agent said, "let him know that I've got my people here watching the race, and depending on how she runs, they're talking about up to five hundred thousand dollars—if she runs the way we think she'll run."

Tebbutt saved the message—a portion of which was later replayed during a lengthy feature segment on Tim and Lisa, produced by the Television Games Network (TVG), a broadcast company devoted to coverage of the racing industry—and holstered his phone.

The race itself was a virtual replay of Lisa's first two starts, albeit at a slower pace. Given the longer distance, Elaine Castillo had been advised to take the horse out carefully, making sure that she broke free but did not bolt so quickly to the front that she would burn herself out. A lot of horses can run six furlongs without any problem, and Lisa had shown herself to be among that group; whether she could run a mile of more was yet to be determined. It was up to Castillo to give the filly every chance to prove herself.

Sent off at 2-5 odds in a cozy, five-horse field, Lisa found herself once again running under nearly perfect conditions: overcast skies and a dry, fast track. She broke cleanly and went to the front, setting a conservative pace, with Castillo smartly holding her in hand and hitting the first quarter mile in nearly twenty-five seconds—a virtual jog for a filly who had demonstrated so much speed in her first two races. It was a sound strategy, executed perfectly by the rider, who guided Lisa through the half in forty-nine seconds, a length in front of the field. Then, deep into the backstretch, Castillo chirped at her mount and asked for a slight shifting of gears; Lisa responded effortlessly. As they rounded the final turn, Lisa's lead had widened to three lengths, and she cruised down the homestretch comfortably, pulling away to an 8 ½-length victory over runner-up Love Our Grandkids. As in their previous two outings, Castillo had encouraged Lisa with her whip only a couple times after the quarter pole.

It simply wasn't necessary.

"Lisa's Booby Trap—a perfect three-for-three!" declared the track announcer as the big horse strode powerfully beneath the wire. "And this is a beautiful filly. Lisa's Booby Trap—very exciting!"

Her winning time was 1:43.3—if not quite as impressive as she'd been at six furlongs, it was still a solid effort, given the fact that it was her first trip over the distance and that she hadn't been pushed by either her rider or the other horses in the field. What mattered most was that Lisa had raced three times in five weeks and won all three times, by a combined margin of 36¾ lengths. She was fast and sound; she was a natural runner and competitor.

By all indications, and against all odds and expectations, she was a prodigious racehorse, having metamorphosed from bust to blue chip seemingly overnight.

After the race, Tebbutt said, the bloodstock agent called

again, this time to confirm his client's bid. They wanted to fly up to New York and close the deal over dinner and drinks. Tebbutt pulled Tim aside and told him of the latest offer for Lisa's Booby Trap.

"They want the horse," Tebbutt said. "And they'll pay a half-million dollars for her."

There was silence as Snyder took in the full weight of that number.

A half-million dollars . . .

"You're full of shit," he finally responded.

Tebbutt shook his head. "No, Timmy. I'm serious."

With that, Tebbutt pulled out his cell phone and dialed up his voice mail. He waited for the bloodstock agent's voice, and then put the call on speaker. Tebbutt let the message play out, then tried to read his friend. It usually wasn't hard, since Tim rarely kept his feelings to himself. Now, though, he seemed at a loss for words.

"Well . . . what do you want to do?" Tebbutt asked.

Tim muttered something inaudible under his breath and walked out of the barn. For the next half hour he paced up and down the shedrow, talking to himself, working up a lather, sometimes gesticulating at no one in particular. Finally, he returned, his shirt soaked with sweat, his cap askew, his angular face pale and drawn.

"Call that guy back," Tim said. "Tell him to save the plane trip. She ain't for sale."

Chapter Thirteen

SARATOGA SPRINGS, NY
SUMMER 2010

There's a subtle difference between age and maturity. With maturity comes confidence and perspective; with age comes fear—palpable if not paralyzing.

In the days and weeks following her impressive string of victories at Finger Lakes Race Track, Lisa's Booby Trap spent much of her time standing quietly in her stall, munching on hay and nuzzling visitors, an athlete waiting patiently for her coach to make a decision about what she would do next. Common sense suggested a change in venue. What was left for her at Finger Lakes, where she had pummeled the competition and recorded times reflective of a horse that deserved a bigger stage?

No one had to tell any of this to Tim Snyder. By now he had earned more money with Lisa than he had with any other horse he'd ever owned: close to forty thousand dollars.

Not exactly a princely sum by elite thoroughbred standards, but enough to properly compensate all the people who had played a role in his acquiring the horse; enough to settle many old debts, get his insurance and other paperwork in order, and officially don the hat of trainer as well as owner. He'd criss-crossed the country too many times to recount, having worked at just about every track you could imagine. But in his forty-plus years in the business, he'd only been to Saratoga Race Course a few times, as an exercise rider in the mid-1980s. He hadn't been back in a quarter century, and he'd never been there as an owner or trainer.

Now, though, it was summertime, when the New York Racing Association annually shifted its operation from Belmont to the quaint little upstate town in the foothills of the Adirondacks. Paradoxically, for the next six weeks, the sport of thoroughbred horse racing would feel less like the fading, arcane pursuit that it has become than the major league sport it once was. Snyder once dreamed of taking a horse to Saratoga, where the smallest purse on a midweek card typically exceeded the weekend feature races at Finger Lakes, and where folks would sometimes stand ten-deep at the rail to watch the greatest horses and jockeys and trainers in the game. Truthfully, though, he'd long ago abandoned that dream, put it aside in favor of more sensible goals, like putting gas in his car and food on the table.

You get to a certain point in life where it's not merely impractical to keep tilting at windmills, but downright embarrassing. A young man's reach should exceed his grasp; an older man knows better. He has a place in life, and he accepts it. Tim Snyder knew his place: on the backstretch of Finger Lakes Racetrack, with its modest crowds and modest purses and modest but fervent gamblers; working with horses that had been modestly bred and cheaply acquired. There were exceptions, and these horses—"shippers," in the parlance of the game—would sometimes make the trek to the big time, to Saratoga or Belmont, but usually they stayed only briefly, and avoided the more competitive stakes races.

Even this, though, had proved elusive to Snyder. Talent and knowledge notwithstanding, he was a career bush leaguer. But now, at age fifty-six, he found himself in the unlikely position of getting called up to the majors, and frankly, the proposition was overwhelming.

"Scared the shit out of me," Snyder recalled. "Saratoga . . . it's the best racing you can find. I'd never been there [as a trainer], didn't know anyone. It was kind of hard to believe."

As was his habit, Tim fretted incessantly about whether or not he should take Lisa to Saratoga, and discussed the horse's options with almost anyone who would listen. Really, though, he was just thinking out loud; there were only a few people whose opinions he valued.

"We had tons of conversations about going to Saratoga," said John Tebbutt, who had grown up in a suburb of Albany, just a half hour from the racetrack, and thus was indoctrinated into the track's lore and culture at a very young age. "Bottom line? It was the right thing for the horse. I offered to give him some money, but by that time he didn't need it. Lisa had won enough money that they could afford to go. There really wasn't any excuse not to go."

Tim heard essentially the same thing from his mother-in-law; his father-in-law was a more pragmatic sort and was still having trouble getting over the notion that Tim had turned down a half-million-dollar offer for the horse. But Frank Calley, too, figured that as long as Tim was going to keep her, he might as well race her. And if he was going to race her, then why not race her at Saratoga? Tim's sister encouraged him, as well.

And then, of course, there was Lisa Calley.

Some nights Tim would drive by the cemetery and shout through the open window: "Hey, hon, we did it again! Won another race!"

Sometimes he'd stop by and have a drink while sitting at her gravesite. He'd talk about his day, and what he'd done, and how he'd stumbled across this incredible horse that had changed his life, and how much the filly meant to him. And how he wished that Lisa could be there with him now to share it all.

More than once, he spent the night.

Then, sometimes, he'd be mucking out the filly's stall or walking her out to the track, or just sitting beside her in a chair, reading the *Daily Racing Form*, when he'd catch himself talking to her in much the same way that he talked with Lisa. And he'd laugh.

People are gonna think I'm nuts.

Or not . . .

"Timmy has always been great with horses," Carol Calley said, "but this was different. This horse really responded to him. When she was at our house, in the barn, she'd start making noise as soon as Timmy's car drove up. At the track she'd dance around when he came to her stall."

Maybe it was all nonsense. Maybe if you miss someone badly enough, you simply find a way to keep them in your life, projecting their spirit and influence wherever it seems to do the most good.

"I would never say that this horse is my daughter," Carol Calley said, laughing at the inherent preposterousness of the suggestion. "But there are times when she does remind me of Lisa. And I do know that she would have loved going to Saratoga, and being part of all that."

In early July, Snyder began making arrangements to ship his horse to Saratoga. Although he had no financial stake in the horse, nor any official designation as trainer, Tebbutt helped his friend plan the trip. Trainers typically rent stall space at Saratoga for the duration of the meet, and shippers either come in for the day or take whatever transient housing is available. Tim was fussy about his filly and considered neither of these options acceptable. If he was going to bring Lisa's Booby Trap to Saratoga, he wanted to settle in early, get comfortable, and maybe run once or twice—preferably in races that would allow her to compete against horses of her own age and gender, for a substantial amount of money.

Tebbutt assisted Snyder in all of this. He arranged a transport van, contacted the stall coordinator and stakes coordinator, and pitched the *idea* of Lisa's Booby Trap, as much as he pitched the horse itself.

"There is no other track like Saratoga," Tebbutt said. "It's an exclusive club. But they took Tim in, gave him space and treated him like royalty. And they did it because they recognized a great story."

Tim and Lisa arrived in Saratoga on July 21, 2010, two days before the track's 142nd season of racing. The filly was assigned a space in the stakes barn, an unassuming gray structure with roughly twenty stalls, located just off Nelson Avenue and only a few hundred yards from both the paddock area and one of the track's two primary public entrances. Although potentially a high-traffic area, the stakes barn was usually quiet and overlooked, for it was far from the bustling backstretch and the sprawling operations of the sport's more prominent trainers. The stakes barn typically housed horses that had shipped to Saratoga for a particular race, and their visits rarely extended beyond a week. As the name suggests, it was elite housing reserved for horses of a certain stature—those that would compete in stakes races. Lisa's Booby Trap, who had been entered in the Grade 1 Coaching Club American Oaks on July 24, met all the obvious criteria, but her visit was open-ended.

As was her trainer's visit.

Like Lisa, Tim needed a place to stay. Trainers, owners, and jockeys who come to Saratoga in July and August face exorbitant seasonal rental rates that can soar as high as five to ten thousand dollars per week for a well-appointed home within walking distance of the track, or in one of the tonier developments near Saratoga Lake. Nightly hotel rates during this period can easily rival those found in New York or Boston.

For Tim Snyder, this was a prohibitive expenditure. And even if he had the money, he wouldn't have spent it.

"They asked me if I needed a room," Tim recalled. "I said, 'Yeah, I'd like to stay with my horse.'"

So he wound up in a tack room above the stakes barn. A small and simple space, but clean and well-ventilated; throw open a window and the breeze would rush right over him. At night he could hear the post-track revelry from Siro's Restaurant, located just up the street. He could also hear Lisa clomping around in her stall. Tim was a restless sleeper; this way, if the mood struck him, he could walk down the stairs in the middle of the night, pull up a chair, and sit beside her.

Although he projected to reporters a refreshing air of confidence and openness, Tim was actually bubbling with anxiety in those first few days at Saratoga.

"He didn't really want to go," said Tebbutt. "I don't know if it would be right to say he was intimidated, but he was . . . it just wasn't in his comfort zone to go to a place like Saratoga. Timmy is a terrific horseman who can handle just about any situation—I think he proved that—but he was out of his element up there. Four days after he got to Saratoga he called me and said, 'You gotta get a van and get me out of here!' Five minutes later he's calling back saying, 'God, I love it here. This is the best track I've been at; how do you guys deal with Finger Lakes?' Five minutes later he's calling again, saying, 'I can't take it here!' For a while he was just overwhelmed."

Reassurance came from a seemingly unlikely source, in the person of Don Hunt, who had sold Lisa's Booby Trap to Tim. While Hunt had a long and sometimes tumultuous relationship with Tim, and while he would soon take offense to the way he felt he was portrayed by the media (and by Tim) in the telling of Lisa's story, he was quick to offer a few words of encouragement when Snyder called him in Florida.

"Can you believe this, Donny?" Snyder said. "I'm in Saratoga, and I'm gonna run a Grade 1."

"Good for you, Timmy. You've got as good a shot as anyone. Don't let them scare you."

"Yeah, I guess," Snyder said. "At least we'll find out what she's worth, huh?"

Sensing the nervousness in Snyder's voice, Hunt offered up one of sport's great truisms, with a slight twist.

"Hey, those big trainers? They put their pants on the same way you do. Saddle their horses the same way, too."

Maybe so, but you couldn't walk along the backstretch of Saratoga, past the pristine and well-stocked and neatly appointed stables of Todd Pletcher or Hall of Famer D. Wayne Lukas, both of whom had horses entered in the Oaks, and not come away with the distinct impression that their saddles were, oh . . . *nicer*. They were among racing's elite, insiders with hordes of assistants and grooms and exercise riders, scores of horses in training at any given time, and a plethora of well-heeled clients who were happy (or at least willing) to pay for it all.

Tim Snyder was an owner-trainer with one horse and no assistant. For all his years in the racing business, he couldn't have been more of an outsider, or more of a longshot. And he knew it. He was also okay with that status.

"I kept telling myself, anything is possible if you put your mind to it," Snyder said. "The racetrack teaches you that anything can happen. Great horses lose, average horses win. I was really nervous about going to Saratoga, going up against all those big trainers, fitting in. Everybody told me I needed a suit for Saratoga. Well, shit, I don't even own a suit, and I wasn't about to buy one just for Saratoga. I basically just went up there and did what I normally do. I got nothing to hide."

Nothing to hide, but maybe something to prove, and the Oaks, a $250,000 race for three-year-old fillies, would certainly provide him with that opportunity. Despite the fact that she had been assigned odds of 30-1, advance press surrounding the race focused heavily on Lisa's Booby Trap and her old-school trainer, setting the stage for Tim Snyder's fifteen minutes of fame.

Unfortunately, the fickle upstate weather did not cooperate, producing torrential downpours on Friday, July 23, that turned the mile-and-an-eighth Spa oval to mud and substantially thinned the fields for most races. That afternoon Snyder made several treks from the stakes barn to the main track, and with each trip he became more concerned about the potential for a sloppy surface the following day, when Lisa was scheduled to run. By evening he had made up his mind: Lisa's Booby Trap would be scratched. The filly had a history of physical problems and had never raced on anything but an ideal surface. Snyder was not above taking a chance once in a while—hell, he'd done it repeatedly over the years—but this was different. This was a unique horse and a once-in-a-lifetime opportunity.

He wasn't about to screw it up.

"It cost me twenty-five hundred dollars to scratch her," Tim said. "That's the nomination fee, and if you don't run, you lose it. A lot of people were disappointed she scratched, but I knew the track wouldn't dry out, and I wasn't sure whether Lisa could run in the mud. I couldn't risk it. I got a one-eyed horse with bad feet, running in a Grade 1 stake at Saratoga, against serious competition, with a lot of money on the line. I'm gonna ask her to do that in the mud? No way you ask that. Don't embarrass the horse, don't get her hurt. She don't deserve that. And anyway, there were a lot of other races to run."

As it happened, the skies cleared on Saturday morning, and by late afternoon, when the field for the Oaks assembled in the gate, the track had dried out. Officially it was listed as "fast," exactly the type of surface that suited Lisa best, and Tim could do nothing but watch as Devil May Care, trained by Todd Pletcher and ridden by John Velasquez, galloped to a four-length victory. This was the first time that the Oaks had been contested at Saratoga—it had traditionally been held downstate at Belmont, but an expanded Spa calendar prompted a change—and it seemed appropriate that the winner was trained by one of Saratoga's most accomplished trainers, and ridden by its most successful jockey. This was the way things were supposed to be. Whether Tim Snyder could have altered the status quo was, for now, a question left unanswered.

When entries for the Coaching Club American Oaks were announced, Elaine Castillo had been named as the jockey for Lisa's Booby Trap. In reality, though, she had already lost the mount to Kent Desormeaux, a troubled but undeniably gifted jockey with a glittering résumé.

As sometimes happens when a horse becomes successful, greater opportunities present themselves to both the horse and its owner and trainer. It's not unusual for a horse in ascendance to lose a lesser-known rider and gain a more prestigious one. Certainly this is what happened with Lisa's Booby Trap, although precisely how it occurred is a matter of conjecture. Riders lose mounts for all sorts of reasons, and most accept it as a part of the game; they can't afford to take it personally or hold a grudge without risking further employment opportunities. It's a small world; people talk.

Nevertheless, Castillo does not hesitate to acknowledge her disappointment over losing the assignment on Lisa's Booby Trap.

"By the time they left Finger Lakes, we knew Lisa was a very good horse," Castillo said. "I tried everything I could to stay on her for Saratoga, and Timmy kept saying 'Yes, yes, yes. She's yours.' I should have known better. But I did my best anyway, and so did my agent. I told Tim I would go to Saratoga and gallop her, work her, do whatever he needed. I really kissed his butt, and I'd never have imagined doing that before this filly came along. I wanted him to know that I was willing to go to Saratoga, even though I was still riding at Finger Lakes. It's a wonderful track and I know a lot of people there. I said I'd go on weekends or whenever I had a day off. But I never made it up there, so I don't know exactly what happened. I just know there are a lot of big riders with big agents at Saratoga, and they get most of the mounts. Then Kent Desormeaux comes along, and well . . . who's going to say no to that?"

As is usually the case in breakups, there are (at least) two sides to the story. Snyder's recollection of the events leading up to the change in jockeys differs from Castillo's. It is his contention that Castillo, who had a steady stream of work at

Finger Lakes, was unwilling to compromise her business by traveling to Saratoga in July and August.

"I told Elaine she could ride the horse at Saratoga if she would come down and breeze her first," Snyder said. "She wanted to pay someone else to breeze the horse for her, and then come in for the race. Well, shit, that ain't the way it works for me. I just felt like she wanted to take the easy way out, so I told her I'd make my own arrangements."

The day after arriving at Saratoga, Snyder ran into Desormeaux during morning workouts. The two talked for a while, with Snyder hinting that the upstart filly might be available, perhaps on opening weekend, when she was slated to run in the Oaks.

"Breeze her for me, see what you think," Snyder told Desormeaux. The jockey galloped Lisa, liked what he felt (and what he'd heard, since like any seasoned rider he had done his homework and knew all about the big filly in the stakes barn), and agreed to take the job.

John Tebbutt watched this scenario unfold from a distance, as he had remained at Finger Lakes, where he had a full stable of horses competing over the summer months. At the time, he did not question Snyder's decision, either publicly or privately. It bothered him to see one of his favorite riders left behind, but Tebbutt understood the nature of the business, especially at the level now occupied by Lisa's Booby Trap.

"Elaine's feelings were hurt," Tebbutt said. "I supported Tim in whatever he did because he was calling the shots. It was his horse. And it is difficult in that situation, when you have a big horse and a rider like Kent becomes available. The stakes are high. But Elaine knew that horse awfully well."

To the casual observer, the hiring of Kent Desormeaux might have seemed like a no-brainer for Snyder. One of only three jockeys (the others being Steve Cauthen and Chris Mc-Carron) to win the Eclipse Award for outstanding rider as both an apprentice and veteran rider, Desormeaux had ridden three Kentucky Derby winners, and in 1998 had come within a nose of winning the Triple Crown aboard one of them (Real Quiet). The Louisiana native had won more than five thousand races and owned the record for most wins by a jockey in a single year. In terms of career earnings, only four other jockeys ranked ahead of him. He'd guided winners in the Preakness Stakes, Belmont Stakes, and Breeders Cup; he'd also won the Travers Stakes in 2009 aboard Summer Bird, so obviously he was no stranger to Saratoga. Along the way he'd been inducted into the National Museum of Racing and Hall of Fame in 2004.

In sum, whenever anyone talked about the best jockeys in the history of the sport, Kent Desormeaux was in the conversation.

But he did not come without baggage.

By the time he was introduced to Lisa's Booby Trap, Desormeaux was forty years old, not over-the-hill by jockey standards, but certainly within view of the summit. He had faced mounting criticism in recent years for what appeared to be mystifying tactics in big races—for example, holding back Big Brown and easing him in the stretch of the Belmont Stakes when the colt had a chance to become the first Triple Crown winner in more than three decades. There was also his disturbing personal behavior. Long known for being a feisty, temperamental competitor with a prickly personality,

Desormeaux was suspended in early July 2010 after failing a breathalyzer test at Woodbine Racetrack in Canada. Desormeaux had flown in from New York to ride a horse called Hold Me Back in the Dominion Day Handicap, but forefeited the mount to another rider. Hold Me Back won anyway, and Desormeaux tried to downplay the incident, claiming he'd merely had a single drink at a party the previous night, an explanation accepted by virtually no one within the racing community, where substance abuse had long been speculated as a reason for Desormeaux's erratic behavior. Indeed, not long after that incident, the jockey acknowledged that he was seeking treatment for an alcohol problem.

And now, just a few weeks later, he was at Saratoga, not so much hustling for work but trying to rebuild his reputation. Riding Lisa's Booby Trap, a horse sure to attract attention whenever she got to the track, was part of that process. But if others were wary of using Desormeaux, Tim Snyder was not.

"I don't give a shit about a guy's issues," he said. "My dad was a rider. I know they drink. I know they do coke. I know they do other things. They can do whatever the hell they want to do as long as they do it right for me. Kent knows his business, and he liked this horse. I wasn't worried."

By the time Lisa's Booby Trap made it to the starting gate at Saratoga on Friday, August 6, 2010, in the $75,000 Loudonville Stakes, she was deep into the process of becoming a pop culture phenomenon, her story having transcended the normally insular world of horse racing. As a result, Tim Snyder's life had taken on a surreal quality. And it was about to get even weirder.

Granted, the six-furlong Loudonville Stakes was not the equivalent of the Coaching Club American Oaks. It was a small overnight stakes race, with a comparatively moderate purse. Still, it wasn't exactly like running at Finger Lakes, either. The field of five horses for the Loudonville included one (Nonna Mia) that was trained by Todd Pletcher, and another (Stormandaprayer) that was owned by celebrity chef and ubiquitous Saratoga fan Bobby Flay. Oddsmakers looked at this group and assigned Lisa's Booby Trap a morning line of 12-1. Betting odds, though, are fluid, reflecting not just the likelihood of a horse winning, but the amount of currency wagered on her. A morning line of 12-1 might indicate that a horse's background and résumé will not provoke bettors to rush to the window in support of her. In the case of Lisa's Booby Trap, though, that is exactly what happened.

At Saratoga, more so than at any other racetrack, the crowd is composed largely of casual fans, tourists who come for the atmosphere and the party and the pageantry, many of whom have neither the expertise nor the inclination to handicap a race. It's easier (and maybe a whole lot more fun) to choose a horse based on some ridiculous, half-baked connection to its name or number or the color of its silks, or because you like the jockey, or because maybe, perhaps, the horse winked at you in the paddock (although it probably was simply trying to shoo away a fly). There are serious, knowledgeable racing fans at Saratoga, to be sure, folks who devour the *Racing Form* and memorize speed figures, but there aren't enough of them to fuel the Saratoga experience. On August

6, in a crowd of 22,383, they were overwhelmed by unscientific, sentimental handicappers who relentlessly drove down the odds on Lisa's Booby Trap and made her a 3-2 favorite by race time.

She rewarded them for betting with their hearts as well as their heads.

"What an amazing day," recalled John Tebbutt, who helped Snyder saddle the filly in the paddock. "The race, the way the crowd responded . . . It sent shivers down my spine."

He wasn't alone. When the starting gate opened, the crowd roared, only to fall silent as Lisa practically stood in the gate and found herself dead last, trailing by six lengths at the quarter-mile mark, reached in a blistering 21 $^{2}/_{5}$ seconds by pacesetter Stormandaprayer. A six-furlong race is a veritable sprint, with only one turn to negotiate and little room for error. Break poorly or wait too long to make a move and you can quickly run out of real estate.

After sitting on the early pace, though, Desormeaux urged Lisa through the turn, taking the filly four wide as they reached the half-mile mark in 44.54 seconds. By the top of the stretch she was in fourth place and running furiously as the rest of the field, weakened from the early, lung-searing effort, came back to her.

"Here comes Lisa's Booby Trap!" shouted track announcer Tom Durkin as the crowd roared its approval.

Meanwhile, all alone in a corner of the clubhouse beneath the grandstand, watching the race on a monitor, was Tim Synder, dressed in cowboy boots, faded jeans, and a Western-style shirt, looking less like an owner at Saratoga Race Course than a backstretch groom or maintenance worker. While some 22,000 people stood in the stands or tried to push their way trackside to watch the race in person, the owner and trainer of Lisa's Booby Trap witnessed the biggest race of his life mostly on a thirty-two-inch television screen.

"That's Timmy," Tebbutt said with a laugh. "He always does that. He likes to be alone when the race goes off."

As he heard the crowd cheering, Snyder stepped out from beneath the grandstand and inched his way toward the rail, maybe twenty meters beyond the finish line. He could see Lisa running wide, running hard. Although he had bet two grand on his own horse the last time she ran at Finger Lakes, he'd stayed away from the window today. Didn't want to jinx her. There was enough pressure as it was.

"My vantage point was terrible—head on," Tim said. "But I knew. I just knew. Man, she was flying!"

The filly swept easily into second place, then took the lead midway through the stretch and galloped to the wire looking strong and poised, six lengths in front of runner-up Nonna Mia and jockey John Velazquez. So sure was Desormeaux of his filly's kick that he used his whip only once after taking the lead, guiding her across the line under a virtual hand ride in a time of 1:09.64.

Tim Snyder tried to push his way to the winner's circle as the crowd stood and cheered. He was lost in a sea of people, none of them even slightly aware that he was the owner of the horse, the trainer of the horse. He was the one who had made this happen, and yet now he couldn't even get to her.

"I actually got punched trying to get through the crowd,"

Snyder recalled. "I was pushing people out of the way and this drunk guy smacked me, called me a little bastard! Jesus, it was my horse; I just wanted to see her."

Moments later Tim reached the winner's circle; Carol Calley was already there, tears falling from beneath her sunglasses. They hugged, Tim gave her a kiss on the cheek, and the two of them stood beside Lisa's Booby Trap as the crowd responded with a nearly endless standing ovation. Then Tim took the reins and walked back up the track, a phalanx of reporters carrying notebooks and digital recorders and video cameras trailing in his wake, hanging on his every word.

"I appreciate y'all taking an interest in my horse," Snyder told them, "but I gotta get her back to the barn."

Shortly thereafter the media turned to Desormeaux for a bit of perspective, and the jockey was only too happy to oblige. Perhaps owing to his Cajun upbringing, Desormeaux was quick to embrace not only the filly he'd just ridden, but the mystical story surrounding her.

"[Tim's] late wife told him that she wanted to come back as a racehorse, and here she is, living vicariously through Lisa's Booby Trap," Desormeaux told reporters. "As far as we believe, she's inside—they have the same heart, and she's carrying this horse. I know how fast she is, and for them to clear her, I knew they had to be smoking. Still and all, though, she came and got them while they were running, so she's of great talent, there's no doubt.

"This is what sport offers," Desormeaux added. "You can amass hero status through the racing industry; this is a perfect example."

That evening, for the first time since he'd been at Saratoga, Tim Snyder left the stakes barn for more than a few minutes. He strolled down Nelson Avenue with a couple friends and turned into Siro's. There he remained, deep into the early morning hours, enjoying the first sweet taste of celebrity and success. Lisa's Booby Trap had earned $42,000 for winning the Loudonville Stakes, but her owner, suddenly lifted out of obscurity, did not even have to reach for his wallet.

"I ended up getting plowed that night," Tim said. "Had chips lined up all over the bar. No one would let me buy a drink."

Chapter Fourteen

With a Saratoga stakes victory came a deepening of Lisa's story, and a broadening of its appeal. Calls came from Hollywood and New York, talk of book deals and movies. *Dateline NBC* shadowed the trainer for the better part of a week to gather footage and interviews for a proposed one-hour special. The national media jumped on a story that tugged at the heartstrings and transcended sports.

Through it all Tim Snyder remained charmingly unfazed. He spent nearly every waking moment at the side of his filly; even the non-waking moments found him just a short flight of stairs away. There was no way to know how the story would end, how high in class the once unwanted filly would climb before bumping up against the ceiling. It seemed impossible to think of her as Breeders Cup material, but still there were rumblings.

"All I know is, we haven't seen the best of her yet," Desormeaux predicted after Lisa's victory in the Loudonville. "This is the best story in horse racing, and it's going to get even better."

Everyone loves a fairy tale, and the story of Lisa's Booby Trap was a good one. That it was somewhat more complicated and less Disneyesque than it appeared on the surface did nothing to diminish interest or squelch fan support. Both horse and trainer were underdogs. Theirs was a tale of life and live, of second chances and hope.

Who isn't a sucker for that? If you couldn't root for Tim Snyder, well, you had no heart.

"I'm actually glad it turned out the way it did," said Ocala Stud's Michael O'Farrell. "We didn't do particularly well when we had this horse. John Shaw didn't do particularly well with her. Don Hunt didn't do particularly well with her. But this Snyder fellow up in New York—who I've never met, incidentally—he did well; he got her to run. That's what the industry is all about. It's a wonderful story for everyone."

Well, maybe not quite.

When Lisa's Booby Trap crossed the finish line first in the Loudonville, Elaine Castillo was a couple hundred miles away, in the jockeys' room at Finger Lakes. She had two mounts that day, in races with combined purses of $21,000. She finished sixth in one race, seventh in the other. Neither of her horses would ever be confused with Lisa's Booby Trap, nor any other horse you were likely to see at Saratoga. It was a long and hard day for Castillo, further complicated when she heard of the minor miracle that had occurred in Saratoga.

"I'll be honest—when I saw her win, it broke my heart

completely," Castillo said. "I had done so much of the work on that horse. It would have been my chance to move up a little bit, too. Instead, it kind of did the opposite for me. I knew better, but it still killed me. It pissed me off, broke my spirit a little. I became kind of resentful and I just quit, eventually. Took like a year off. I won't blame it all on what happened with Tim and Lisa, but that was a big part of it. All of us in the game work so hard and deal with so much. We all take the disappointment differently. Some can put up with it more. I was in a bad mood and resentful, and that's not who I wanted to be."

By the end of the summer Castillo had withdrawn entirely from the sport. She stopped going to the track, wouldn't even work horses, let alone race them. She spent a few months in Italy "clearing my head, getting all that craziness out of my mind," before eventually coming back to the States and trying to rebuild her career. She loved horse racing too much to stay away from it forever. While Castillo said she bears no grudge against Tim Snyder, the pain will never disappear completely.

"Other trainers do it all the time. It's part of the game," Castillo said. "But that doesn't make it not hurt. The thing is, the big trainers get away with this, and everyone accepts it. I was thinking, Who the hell is Timmy Snyder? And that's not a good way to be. We get along fine now. I just try to keep a good, professional relationship and move forward. But I know I'll never ride that filly again."

For the shortest time imaginable, Lisa's Booby Trap was the biggest name in horse racing. She was an equine version of Jeremy Lin, the overlooked and unwanted point guard who in February 2012 came seemingly out of nowhere—"nowhere" in this case being Harvard, and then the far end of the New York Knicks' bench—to become, for a moment, the most popular player, and the very best story, the NBA had to offer. Like Lin, Lisa was a comet, provoking unreasonable expectations for both longevity and light.

The offers kept coming and Tim Snyder kept turning them down, which only served to enhance the appeal of the story. Whether Tim was a man of enormous integrity or foolishness, whether his commitment to Lisa was fueled primarily by devotion to his wife or devotion to his own ego and arrogance, was batted about both privately and publicly in racing circles. One of the last offers was also one of the best, according to John Tebbutt. It came from Michael Dubb, a well-known and successful horseman who would saddle more winners than any other owner at Saratoga in 2010. Knowing of Snyder's reluctance to part ways with Lisa, at any cost, Dubb offered Snyder $150,000 for half ownership, Tebbutt said.

It seemed the ideal arrangement, permitting a long-broke trainer and owner to put some much-needed coin in his pocket, while also maintaining both a future revenue stream and a personal connection to the filly that had changed his life. He would have money; he would make more money; and he would still be involved with the horse.

Tebbutt fielded the offer and took it to Snyder.

"Tell him thanks, but no thanks," Tim said. "She's my horse."

Finally, according to Tebbutt, came an offer of $250,000

from another owner who said he would allow Snyder to keep the filly, and any purses she earned, through three more starts—even after money had changed hands.

Again, Tim declined.

"Everyone thought I was ignorant for not taking the money, but I just would have gone on a spending spree, the way I always do when I get a little cash," Snyder would later explain (or rationalize). "And the longer I had the horse, the closer we became; the more it felt like my wife was getting involved in her. Lisa, my wife, she had all kinds of physical problems, but she was a good person. And this filly . . . she struck me a lot like my wife, and the longer I was around her, the more they seemed similar."

Perhaps recognizing that he was treading dangerously close to the sort of territory he had been careful to avoid, Tim pulled back just a bit.

"Look, the horse wasn't a replacement for my wife, but I needed something to keep me going. I didn't have no girl-friend, didn't want one either. I'd rather have the horse, to be honest with you. She's a moneymaker and we get along. I get up in the morning, I feed her, I take care of her, I talk to her. She's happy and I'm happy.

"I think I conquered this horse because I spent so much time with her and I learned how to communicate with her. And sometimes I talk to her just like I talked to my old lady, kind of harsh, know what I mean? Basically that's how I am. It's not an act. Some people don't like it; they're not used to hearing somebody that rough cut. But I tell it like it is, and Lisa appreciated that. She accepted me for who I am. Me and my wife had our ups and downs like any other married couple, but we settled all our arguments before we went to bed. We didn't cheat on each other and we didn't lie to each other. We took care of each other. She'd fight with me, all right—by my side! I remember a guy one time wouldn't pay us the money he owed after we'd shipped horses for him. We got in a big argument and the son of a bitch took a swing at me. Before I could even react Lisa had picked up a feed bucket and hit him over the head with it. How many wives defend their husbands that way?"

Well . . . probably not very many. And if you come across some semblance of that spirit, that spark, you latch onto it. No matter where it happens to be.

"That horse gave Timmy his life back," said Tebbutt. "He couldn't give her up."

Nearly a month would pass before Lisa's Bobby Trap ran her next race, as Tim Snyder carefully weighed his options and opportunities. He had initially considered pointing the filly toward the $100,000 Grade 3 Victory Ride Stakes in the final week of the meet, but those plans changed on August 18, when Snyder took her out for a morning gallop on the turf course at the Oklahoma Track, a busy training and stabling facility located just across Union Avenue from the main entrance to Saratoga Race Course.

Lisa's Booby Trap was not a grass runner, and Snyder had no intention when he woke that morning of trying to make her one. While some racehorses demonstrate little regard for the type of surface on which they compete (dirt or grass), far more typical is the animal that clearly prefers one surface over another. Oftentimes this proclivity can be seen deep into a horse's bloodlines: if the mare is a turf horse, for example, then it's likely her offspring will also be quicker on turf. In Lisa's case, there was nothing in her lineage to indicate that she would adapt well to a grass course, and Snyder had smartly chosen to train and race her on dirt from the very beginning. With extraordinary results.

Sometimes, though, a trainer will work a horse on grass simply as a change of pace, or to give her some training time on a surface that is softer and supposedly more forgiving. In reality, though, a turf course, which is often uneven and pitted, can be more challenging to a horse.

Not to mention confusing. Eons of evolution have left horses with an instinctive desire to run and the capacity to gallop over a wide variety of surfaces, with grass being the most natural. But if a horse has spent nearly its entire life training on dirt, there is no telling how it will respond to a sudden change, and so caution is generally advised. Indeed, when Kent Desormeaux led Lisa onto the turf course, he was under the impression that he was merely to breeze the filly. At the last moment, Snyder instructed the rider to follow his gut.

"If she likes [the surface] and she wants to run, let her go," the trainer advised.

The result was a brief but impressive workout: officially, three furlongs in 35.27 seconds, although she continued to gallop out and unofficially covered a half mile in 47.2 seconds. To Snyder, she looked like a turf horse. He consulted with Desormeaux, who informed him that the filly had felt strong and confident, and not the least bit squeamish. With that, Tim Snyder, the unconventional trainer with the unconventional horse, diverted once again from conventional wisdom. After four consecutive victories on the dirt, by a combined margin of 42 ¾ lengths, and without a single grass race to her credit, she would run her next race September 2, on the turf. Not only would she be switching surfaces, but she would be running farther. The Victory Ride was a six-furlong race, the same distance at which Lisa had won three of her four starts. Instead, her next start would be at one mile. Ironically, given her trainer's penchant for rolling the dice, the name of the race was the Riskaverse Stakes.

"He wins two or three races and then he puts her on the grass!" noted a befuddled John Shaw. "Like she wasn't doing good enough on the dirt or something. You've got to be retarded to do something like that. She had no grass pedigree at all. None!"

Maybe, though, it was neither foolishness nor stupidity that provoked Snyder's decision, but rather sensitivity. True, when pressed about his motivation for entering Lisa in the Riskaverse, Tim did allude to the possibility that she could make more money as a grass horse. But he also pointed out that given her troubled upbringing and structural deficiencies, maybe she'd be less prone to injury and thus have a longer and healthier career on turf.

If it was a somewhat less conservative approach than might have been displayed by most trainers, it wasn't like he was reinventing the wheel.

Running in the Riskaverse was just . . . well . . . risky.

"I thought Timmy did all the right things with this horse," said Tebbutt. "When you make a change, you never know how it will work out, but she worked so well on the turf. And

Desormeaux is an excellent rider, a great judge of horseflesh. For him to tell Timmy that he should run her on the turf . . . that says a lot. Timmy had input from other people. He didn't just decide on a whim to do this, all on his own."

Tebbutt let out a sigh of exasperation.

"It's so easy to cut people up after the fact; you see it all the time in horse racing. It's a tough business. And it wasn't like Timmy had a string of million-dollar horses to practice on."

As any horseman—or any gambler, for that matter—can attest, there is no such thing as a sure bet. On September 2, Lisa's Booby Trap went off as an even-money favorite (down from a morning line of 5-2) in the Riskaverse Stakes. On the eve of the race Snyder had moved his filly to a more secluded spot on the backstretch, in the hope of gaining some much-needed privacy. This left her with a long and public march to the paddock prior to race time, during which Lisa, trailed by a *Dateline NBC* camera crew, was showered with applause and cheers by a crowd that stood three-deep along the rail. Although attendance on this sweltering (temperatures in the nineties) afternoon was just a shade under ten thousand, modest by Saratoga standards, a significant percentage seemed to have flocked to the walkway to witness the procession of Lisa's Booby Trap. It was, one couldn't help but notice, the type of response generated only by the sport's true stars.

"Go get 'em, girl!"

"Yeah, Lisa!"

The paddock at Saratoga is a charming if somewhat odd

collage of style and personality and conflicting interests. Jockeys and trainers go about the business of preparing for the next race with precisely the appropriate degree of seriousness, while all around them is the pageantry of a day at the races. Ostensibly, paddock access is restricted to those who have some legitimate reason to be there: horsemen, owners, media. In reality, though, the paddock (at Saratoga, anyway) routinely fills with people who have only the slimmest of connections to the horses involved: nephews and nieces of the jockey or trainer; college frat buddies of the owner's son; a wide assortment of friends and relatives and "industry insiders," many wearing searsucker jackets, madras pants, and hats the size of manhole covers (though hopefully not all at the same time).

And that's just inside the gate.

Outside the gate, on a busy day—and there are many of these at Saratoga—a louder and less well-heeled throng encircles the paddock, breaking only when the "riders up" command is given and the jockeys climb aboard their mounts, and the field parades to the track.

Imagine an NFL locker room thrown open to fans and the media just moments before kickoff, and you have some idea of the level of intrusiveness. But it's all part of the game in horse racing and everyone accepts it, with varying degrees of annoyance, as the price of doing business.

As he saddled Lisa's Booby Trap, Tim Snyder seemed oblivious to his surroundings; he might as well have been at Finger Lakes, so focused was he on the task at hand, so disinterested in the growing cluster of fans pointing and gawking at his horse. Not even the presence of family and friends could distract him. And there were more of them in the paddock on this blistering afternoon than Tim had seen in years. His in-laws had made the trip, of course. But so had his sister and his daughter, Sierra, both of whom had flown in from California.

"I'd always known that my brother was a good horseman," said Cheryl Hall. "But to see him there, in Saratoga, and the way he worked . . . it was just amazing. It was like watching a surgeon. He knew exactly what he was doing, and he handled himself so professionally. I couldn't have been more proud of him."

Tim was all business in the paddock. There was a brief handshake and photo op with John Walsh, known primarily as the television host of *America's Most Wanted*, but also an avid horse racing fan and polo player from Central New York who had befriended Snyder; as the race drew near, though, Tim communicated only with Tebbutt and Desormeaux.

Typically, an owner will leave the paddock and retreat to the privacy of a clubhouse box seat when his horse exits the paddock. A trainer might walk to the edge of the track before handing the reins to an assistant and following the owner upstairs. Tim Snyder walked Lisa out of the paddock, through the crowd, and onto the track himself, releasing the reins only when it was time for Desormeaux to warm her up. He offered a few last-second instructions, gave Lisa a pat on the rump, and then disappeared beneath the grandstand.

The Riskaverse was split into two divisions, with Lisa's Booby Trap one of ten three-year-old fillies competing in the ninth race. As she settled into the gate, on the far inside, Desormeaux noticed nothing out of the ordinary. Although it took a while to load the entire field, and she spent considerable time standing in the cage, Lisa seemed relaxed, ready to run. But at 5:32 P.M., when the bell sounded and the door swung open, she hesitated before breaking. It wasn't a fatal error, as Lisa's inside position allowed her to move along the hedge and cover lost ground quickly. She settled into fourth place, five lengths behind frontrunner Queen of the Creek and jockey Julien Leparoux.

At the rail, near the finish line, watching with great concern, was a New York attorney and fellow horse owner named George Santangelo, who had befriended Snyder in the previous month and offered to help him with legal matters. Like most people at Saratoga, Santangelo had fallen for the story of Lisa's Booby Trap and wanted the horse to run well on this day; unlike most people, though, he knew enough about the game to immediately understand the gravity of the situation. As the field raced along the backstretch, and Lisa failed to find her footing, Santangelo shook his head.

"Something's not right," he said. "She's not running."

As the field approached the final turn, with the crowd imploring the filly to shift gears, track announcer Tom Durkin stated the obvious:

"A six-length lead with time starting to tick away. Situation critical for Lisa's Booby Trap."

By that point, Desormeaux had dug into the filly and asked her to run; she gave him nothing in return. Perhaps she was agitated by the change in track surface or discouraged by the withering heat; maybe she'd simply run one too many races. For whatever reason, Lisa never fired. By the time they reached the top of the stretch, Desormeaux, unwilling to risk her health and heart in pursuit of an unattainable goal, eased up on the filly. She crossed the finish line in last place, seventeen lengths behind Queen of the Creek, a wire-to-wire winner.

A smattering of sympathetic applause from a stunned and disappointed crowd greeted Lisa as she walked back toward the finish line after the race. Tim Snyder stepped onto the track and took the horse in hand as Desormeaux dismounted. The two talked briefly, somberly before the rider walked off toward the jockeys' quarters to change into different silks. The ninth race was officially over, and he had another mount in the tenth. Meanwhile, Tim Snyder walked back up the homestretch, alongside his horse, just as he had done one month earlier, with a gaggle of reporters trailing him. This time, though, they peppered him with questions of a different sort.

"What happened?"

"What went wrong?"

"Is she hurt?"

He had no explanation, no satisfactory answer; one by one the reporters fell away, eventually leaving Snyder all alone with his filly as they exited the track and walked toward the "spit barn," where a urine sample of Lisa's would be collected and tested. Standard postrace protocol; for the trainer, though, a whole lot less pleasant when you've just blown up in the biggest race of your life.

Nearly an hour would pass before Snyder and Lisa emerged from the test barn. They stood together near the edge of the track, cars rushing by on Union Avenue just a short distance away as the crowd filtered out after another day of racing. Subdued and a bit perplexed, Snyder struggled for an explanation.

"Maybe she didn't like the grass," he said. "Maybe the heat."

He shrugged.

"Maybe she just needs a break."

Eventually the two of them began walking back toward the stakes barn, where Lisa would spend the next few days before returning either to Finger Lakes or to his mother-in-law's farm—Snyder hadn't yet decided. They moved slowly, in perfect sync, the little trainer and the big filly, each of them sweating profusely, looking tired and beaten by the long day's effort. Snyder was asked if he was disappointed with the filly's performance. It was meant almost as a rhetorical question, and yet, without breaking stride or giving it a moment's thought, Tim ran a hand along Lisa's great, sloping back and smiled.

"This horse could never disappoint me. She don't owe me a thing."

Epilogue

CAMILLUS, NY
FEBRUARY 2011

Winter grips the Finger Lakes region of Central New York hard and fast, closing its fist well before Thanksgiving and not letting go until deep into April. As Tim Snyder walks into the Calley house after running some morning errands, he takes a few heavy steps to knock the snow from his boots. The clattering provokes yelps of protest from T-Bone, the squatty little Jack Russell who serves as unofficial sentry for the family, and who remains Tim's sidekick and companion.

As it has been on and off for nearly twenty years, this rambling, unassuming farmhouse is Tim's home. Only a mile or so down the road are the usual comforts (or trappings, depending on how you look at it) of suburbia—convenience stores, subdivisions, strip malls of chain restaurants and retail outlets—but here, in a rural neighborhood, there is room to

move and to breathe. Room for people of diverse backgrounds, thrown together by circumstance and love. Room
for their complicated and sometimes messy, broken lives to
bump up against each other and intersect. Room for their
dogs and cats and horses.

Especially horses.

"Come on, I'll show you where she lives," Tim tells a
visitor, and soon they are trudging through knee-deep pow-
der, past a handful of cars and trucks awaiting rebirth in the
backyard, past great, twisting heaps of snowcapped deadfall.
The Calleys have several acres of land, and some of it is left
untended, giving the impression of a place that is at once
cozy and overwhelming.

Far in the back are two connected barns. One is cavern-
ous, with a large walking ring and plenty of room to do
some of the hard and rough work of breaking and training
horses. The other barn is smaller, with two short rows of
stalls. As Tim throws open the door on this stark winter morning, sunlight fills the barn. Three horses stand in
their stalls, puffs of steam rising rhythmically from their
nostrils.

Two of the horses are relatively cheap claimers, purchased the previous summer when Snyder had a terrific racehorse and some money in his pocket. The filly whose earnings
led to those purchases is in one of the center stalls. As Snyder's voice fills the barn, she tilts her head to the side in obvious recognition.

"Here she is," Tim says, reaching up to pat her on the
shoulder. "How ya' doin' this morning, girl?"

Lisa's Booby Trap is an impressive physical specimen,

seeming even larger now in the narrow confines of this modest barn than she did on the backstretch at Saratoga. Always tall, she has grown impressively into her body, and when the trainer says she's happy and healthy and will be fit as hell in the spring when Finger Lakes Racetrack opens, you can't help but think maybe he's right.

"I'm telling you right now," Tim predicts, "this filly will be better than ever."

Appearances can be unreliable. Lisa's Booby Trap had always been a beautiful, athletic girl, but only fleetingly was she a filly whose performances matched her aesthetic charm. Three weeks after blowing up in the Riskaverse Stakes, Lisa's Booby Trap found herself in an allowance race at Finger Lakes. Snyder had figured a short race (five and a half furlongs) on the dirt, against light competition, would be just the thing she needed to regain her footing. Instead, she ran an oddly anxious race, ducking out early, bumping another horse, then veering wide before struggling to a third-place finish. At that point Snyder shut her down for the season.

Months went by as Snyder rested the filly, invested in bloodwork to determine whether there was some sort of systemic problem, and slowly went about the task of getting her ready for a comeback. By now, though, Lisa's Booby Trap had become, to most of the racing world, a mere footnote; or, worse, a fluke. Not that she was the first horse to disappear seemingly overnight.

"There's usually a window for horses to run well," noted Michael O'Farrell. "And when it closes, it closes fast."

Even John Tebbutt, in the wake of Lisa's two consecutive losses, was prepared to declare her career over. At the very least, he considered it unlikely that the filly would ever run as well as she had in the summer of 2010.

"I hope so, but I doubt it," Tebbutt said. "A lot of horses peak at that point, in their three-year-old year. Everything is clicking, they're young and healthy. For Lisa, it was perfect for a while there; she was on top of her game. And then . . . well, it's just hard to get them back after something like that. When they start running badly, they're usually done. It's not necessarily because there's anything wrong with them, but this filly had a lot of issues. I think it's amazing that Timmy did what he did with her."

Stubborn to the bone, Snyder would make good on his promise to get Lisa back on the track, if not necessarily *back on track*. In the spring and early summer of 2011 she would win two of three starts at Finger Lakes before returning to Saratoga for the running of the Rachel Alexandra Stakes on August 1. As before, Lisa ran before a crowd that included Tim Snyder's sister and daughter, who had once again flown in from California. For good luck, Carol Calley watched the race while wearing a watch that had belonged to her daughter. If the buzz surrounding Lisa's Booby Trap had diminished considerably this time around, she remained both a fan and bettor's favorite (if only for sentimental reasons), going off as the second choice at 3-1 odds.

In a performance eerily similar to the previous year, though, Lisa struggled badly before a Saratoga crowd that hoped to witness a resurrection of her story, lugging out while running near the front early in the race, and then again as the field approached the final turn. Jockey Dennis Carr, who had picked up the mount on Lisa's Booby Trap at Finger Lakes, struggled mightily to get the filly under control, but she fought him every inch of the way. Fearing his mount might veer into traffic and cause a catastrophic accident, Carr surrendered as they came into the stretch and eased the filly across the line.

She was the eighth finisher in an eight-horse field.

Dead last. Again.

"I couldn't get ahold of her," the jockey said to Snyder as they walked off the track. "Never seen her do that before."

The trainer nodded grimly.

A few weeks and several thousand dollars in vet bills later, Snyder revealed that Lisa had been bothered by both an abscessed tooth (which was removed) and an infection in her eye, the result of dirt having been kicked up in front of her during the Rachel Alexandra. Once healed, she returned to the track—again, at Finger Lakes—and won her next three starts. In November 2011 she was named Horse of the Year at Finger Lakes Racetrack.

In 2012 Lisa ran twice at Presque Isle Downs in Erie, Pennsylvania, and once at Finger Lakes. She hit the board in all three races, but did not win any of them. Lisa's Booby Trap had by now compiled career winnings of $169,580 dollars. If she was no longer on the national radar—no longer the kind of horse that came up in discussions of Eclipse Awards and Breeders Cups—she was nonetheless a solid minor league racehorse.

In ways large and small, she was an earner.

Through the filly Tim Snyder had found purpose and motivation; he'd also reconnected with friends and family. One day, for example, he got a call from his childhood buddy Dale Thirtyacre. The two had drifted apart decades earlier, with Tim working at tracks mostly in the Northeast and Florida, and Dale working in the Midwest. Tim made a life out of the business; Dale did too, for a while, before moving on to other pursuits. Eventually he took a job installing insulation, work that by 2012 had left him on disability, incapacitated by emphysema.

"My brother called me one day," Thirtyacre remembered. "He said Timmy had this great horse. I was surprised to hear that he was even alive. I had no idea."

Thirtyacre stopped speaking for a moment. His breathing was labored, and it sounded for a moment as though he had simply grown too tired to talk any longer. Suddenly, though, he began crying.

"Timmy was like my brother; I thought he was gone forever. And now he was back from the dead."

By the fall of 2012 Lisa's Booby Trap had returned once more to the Calley home in Camillus. Offers to purchase the mare had mostly dried up, and those that occasionally came in were for a fraction of what Snyder had been offered two years earlier. Not that it mattered, for the horse remained off the market, unavailable at any price.

Meanwhile, Tim Snyder, after several years of self-neglect—due primarily to a lack of insurance—began addressing some nagging health problems of his own. Most people had noticed during Lisa's time in the spotlight that the trainer walked with a pronounced limp, a condition he attributed primarily to arthritis and accrued scar tissue from old injuries, but which probably had more to do with the undiagnosed lump mushrooming in his upper leg. There was a persistent cough, too, and pain in his ribs.

Eventually Tim endured the necessary tests and scans, and sat through endless hours of consultations with doctors; he listened with great agitation and annoyance as they recommended a drastic course of treatment. There would be radiation to shrink the tumor, surgery to remove what was left, and then chemotherapy to beat back the metastases on his liver, and in his lymph nodes.

That was the plan, anyway.

Snyder wasn't so sure. The cutting he didn't mind. He'd been through worse. But the chemo? He saw what that had done to his wife and to his father, the way it took them apart, an ounce at a time.

"Fuck that," he said. "They want to pump me full of poison so I can live one more year, and feel like shit the whole time? I'd rather ride it out and maybe have two or three good years. And who the hell knows what'll happen? Doctors don't know everything, right?"

There was a pause, a deep sigh, and then a sudden change of direction.

"Hey, let me tell you something else. I got a damn good horse here. She's resting in my barn, and she's gonna come back next year, strong as hell. She's gonna win another hundred thousand dollars, and then I'm gonna breed her. We ain't done yet. Believe me . . . you ain't heard the last of Lisa's Booby Trap."

Acknowledgments

The writing of a book is a long and frequently lonely journey. But it really isn't a solitary undertaking. The truth is this: on the road from concept to publication, input is required, and gratefully accepted, from numerous contributors.

I'll start with my family, since they have to put up with a writer's obsessiveness, moodiness, and endless sharing of anecdotes that may or may not be of any interest. My wife, Sue, shoulders most of the burden with patience and encouragement, but I owe a debt of gratitude as well to my daughter, Emily, a gifted writer and keen listener, and my son, Max, who knows a good story when he hears one.

Thanks also to my sister, Peg, for support in ways too numerous to recount here, and to my brother, Tim, who is not only an exceptional writer, but one of the most knowledgeable horse-racing journalists in the business. And to my parents for raising all of us in a home where reading mattered and books were seen as a pleasure, not a chore.

The Ghost Horse could not have been written without the full cooperation and trust of Tim Snyder, who opened his life to me, sharing details both pleasant and extraordinarily painful. From the outset, he held nothing back, and his openness made for a richer book than otherwise would have been possible.

Thanks, also, to Carol Calley and Frank Calley, who graciously welcomed me into their home and answered all of my questions, no matter how intrusive. I can't imagine that there is anything more painful for parents to endure than the death of one of their children; and I don't think the hurt is diminished simply because that child has grown into adulthood. By the time I began working on this book, Lisa Calley had been deceased for seven years, but she remained a strong and vivid presence in the Calley home: in photos, trophies, trinkets and other memorabilia, but in spirit as well. To the extent that it's possible to know someone you've never met, I feel like I came to know Lisa, and I have Frank and Carol to thank for that. Like Tim, they trusted me with their most intimate feelings and memories. I hope I honored that trust.

Thanks to George Santangelo, a horse lover who introduced me to Tim and helped facilitate our working relationship. And to John Tebbutt, a racetrack lifer who knows Tim Snyder about as well as anyone, and who helped fill in the gaps of a sometimes murky story.

As always, I owe a debt of gratitude to my agent, Frank

Weimann of the Literary Group, who continues to be a smart and savvy partner while indulging my need to pursue the occasional labor of love.

Finally, thanks to everyone at St. Martin's Press, most notably my editor, Marc Resnick, for having faith in this book, even as the author blew one deadline after another. I appreciate your patience more than you can imagine, and I hope the final product was worth the wait.